THE PRUSSIAN CAMPAIGN OF 1866

A TACTICAL RETROSPECT

Capt Theodor May

Authorised translation from the German by
Col H.A.Ouvry CB (late 9th Lancers)

New Introduction by Duncan Rogers

Helion & Company Ltd

Helion & Company
26 Willow Road
Solihull
West Midlands
B91 1UE
England
Tel. 0121 705 3393
Fax 0121 711 4075
Email: publishing@helion.co.uk
Website: http://www.helion.co.uk

Published by Helion & Company 2006

Originally published by Mitchell & Company, London, 1870

Printed by Henry Ling Ltd, Dorchester, Dorset

ISBN 1 874622 14 0

British Library Cataloguing-in-Publication Data
A Catalogue record of this book is available from the British Library

For details of other military history titles published by Helion & Company contact the above address, or visit our website. We always welcome receiving book proposals from prospective authors working in military history.

Contents

Capt Theodor May

New Introduction by Duncan Rogers

This book was first published as a slim pamphlet in Berlin in 1869. It was immediately set apart from the vast majority of its contemporary publications by its willingness to examine Prussian defeats during the Campaign of 1866, instead of focusing on victories. Hitherto, there had been an unabated rush of *Gedenkblätter, Gedenkbücher* and other hagiographical studies that celebrated the glory of Prussia and its army. Suddenly here was a Prussian officer exposing some of the army's shortcomings. The Prussia of the 1860s was not a liberal country, and "hanging out dirty linen" in public was a brave thing to do. Of course, the German edition was published anonymously.

An English edition followed soon after, and went through three editions in rapid succession. This reprint is of the third English edition. The translator, Colonel Henry Aimé Ouvry, was a respected soldier and author with that wide-ranging taste common to Victorians - he even translated Sanskrit literature under the *nom-de-plume* Satyam Jayati.[1] The prefaces that he wrote to three successive editions are worthy in themselves, and take account of changes in the political and military climate due to the outbreak of the Franco-Prussian War between the publication of the first and second English editions.

In the meantime, the book's publication in Germany had spawned some debate and controversy. In 1869 a pamphlet entitled *Über die preußische Infanterie (On the Prussian Infantry)* appeared, also published anonymously, and seemingly written by the same author as *The Prussian Campaign of 1866.* It too made proposals regarding recommended changes in tactics and organisation.

Whilst the publication of anonymous pamphlets was a common occurrence within military literature of the mid-19th century, the Prussian

1 He also wrote: *Military Government. The case of the Disestablishment and Disendowment of Second Lieutenant-Colonelcies, without compensation to present incumbents; with remarks on the misappropriation of the Reserve Fund* (1867), *The Reserve Fund and the Purchase Corps* (1870), *The Land Question in England Popularly Explained* (1871), *Stein And His Reforms in Prussia* (1873), *Cavalry Experiences and Leaves from My Journal* (1892). As a translator he is credited with *Rita Sanhara, or Assemblage of Seasons* (1867), *The Megha Duta, or Cloud Messenger* (1868), *On Responsibility in War* (1869), *The Prussian Campaign of 1866, a Tactical Retrospect* (1870), *On the Prussian Infantry* (1870), *Précis Of a Retrospect on a Tactical Retrospect; and Reply to the Pamphlet "On the Prussian Infantry of 1866"* (1871), *On the Agricultural Community of the Middle Ages and Inclosures of the 16th Century* (1871), *Studies on the Leading of Troops* (1872), *The Dietetics of the Soul* (1873), *An Unsectarian Catechism of Christian and Social Instruction* (1874).

General Staff in particular felt that the continued appearance of such writings required a reply. In particular, the General Staff were concerned that the readership of such pamphlets might gain the impression that they carried some kind of official stamp, or seal of approval. Likewise, open criticism, even when published anonymously, was frowned upon in Prussia. Thus, in 1870 the General Staff issued their official reply in the book *Précis of a Retrospect on the Tactical Retrospect; and Reply to the Pamphlet "On the Prussian Infantry of 1866"*. The book's author was listed as 'Colonel von Schellendorf'.

'Colonel von Schellendorf' was none other than Oberstlieutenant (Lt Col) Paul Leopold Eduard Anton Heinrich Bronsart von Schellendorf, at that time a Head of Department *(Abteilungschef)* within the General Staff. A talented career officer, he had joined the army in 1845, and during the Campaign of 1866 served as a Major attached to the Staff of the II Armeekorps, seeing combat at Gitschin and Königgrätz. He would later continue to rise in the ranks to become a Lieutenant-General. In his preface to the English edition of von Schellendorf's book, Colonel Ouvry comments:

> This reply... is really a critical examination of the tactical views contained in the Prussian Infantry, and, although bearing the name of a Prussian Colonel, is actually, in so far as the tactical reasoning goes, the work of Count von Moltke.

Fundamentally, there is no reason to disagree with this astute observation, which equally applies to the book *The Prussian Campaign of 1866*. Von Schellendorf was very much a protege of von Moltke, and his work within the General Staff would have exposed him to the latter's views to a high degree.

In his preface, von Schellendorf commented:

> We are convinced that the continual publication of brochures of this character does no good in the long run to the Prussian service. We consider, therefore, that a voice from the Army should be raised against them, and this task has been undertaken in the following pages.

The author of the two pamphlets that caused such a stir within military circles was, like von Schellendorf, a career soldier, Captain Theodor Robert May, an officer serving in the Prussian 44th Infantry Regt.[2] His biographical details make interesting reading.

May was not a Prussian by birth; he was born in Kassel, Hessen-Nassau. He entered the Army in 1853, and during the Campaign of 1866 served, along with his Regiment, at the battle of Trautenau, an action that looms

2 It is interesting to note that the British Library catalogue becomes confused over the authorship of these various pamphlets, and attributes this book to von Schellendorf.

large in his narrative. He was obviously marked out as a talented officer by his superiors, for he spent the best part of seven months at the War Academy during 1867. He then followed this with nearly six months attached to the General Staff. Thus when von Schellendorf writes in the preface to his book, alluding to the identity of the author, "There can be scarcely any doubt that he led a Musketeer Company of the 2nd Infantry Division", he was writing from personal knowledge and almost certainly acquaintance with Captain May. May was killed in action on 27 November 1870, at the Battle of Amiens, during the Franco-Prussian War.

Career details of the author[3]:

27 June 1836	Born Theodor Robert May, in Kassel, Hessen-Nassau.
29 June 1853	Entered the Prussian Army's 29th Infantry Regiment.
10 November 1855	Promoted to Second Lieutenant.
2 August 1862	Transferred to the 44th Infantry Regiment.
22 May 1864	Promoted to First Lieutenant.
1866	Served with his Regiment's 6th Company during the Campaign against Austria. Present at the battles of Trautenau, Königgrätz and Tobitschau. Awarded the Order of the Red Eagle 4th Class with Swords.
8 January-1 August 1867	Seconded to the War Academy.
1 May 1868-9 January 1869	Seconded to the General Staff.
9 January 1869	Promoted to Captain, commander of the Regiment's 6th Company.
27 November 1870	Killed in action at the Battle of Amiens.

It is hoped that the publication of this book not only provides useful contemporary information on the Prussian army and its tactics during the Campaign of 1866, but also highlights the fact that military thought in the 1860s was very much a dynamic force, and not ossified, as it is sometimes portrayed.

3 The details of the author and his military career have been gleaned from *Geschichte des 7. Ostpreußischen Infanterie-Regiments Nr 44 von 1860-1885* by Erich & Toeppen (Berlin, 1885).

Translator's Preface

A few weeks age the anonymous German pamphlet, entitled, "Tacktische Rükblicke auf 1866" fell into the hands of the translator. Its intrinsic merits appeared so extraordinary, and the matter treated of so important, that he thought it might be beneficial to our own officers if it were put in a form accessible to those not conversant with the German language. It treats of the war experiences of the Prussians in 1866, and is written in a truthful and courageous vein, the author speaking out very plainly, and never seeking to hide the shortcomings of his countrymen.

Some however may think that all treatises on the science and art of war are now superfluous, since we learn from the sayings of certain wise men, that we are to have no more wars, and that we are to live for the future in one gigantic, virtuous republic.

This is the opinion of M Victor Hugo; and M Thiers says, "Have as little to do as possible with your neighbour; keep aloof from him; thus you will not be able to make war." Again, M Jules Simon lays down the law thus:

> All join with me in demanding liberty, and with it, its indispensable element, peace: when nations shall become rivals in industry, instead of enemies in arms, try to make war if you can.[1] I defy you to the attempt – upon this freedom of work and commerce, the future of universal liberty is destined to be based, and war shall be no more. (Loud cheering)

This may be all very fine, and no doubt these gentlemen have a right to their opinions; we, however, who know human nature a little better, will leave them to their Utopian visions; for whatever they may say, and however much they may preach, while we are constituted as we are, war will ever be the history of mankind.

In addition to the very instructive tactical considerations which are discussed in this pamphlet, there is one point of most momentous import to us in England at the present time: I mean the example of Prussia.

Humbled to the dust, bleeding at every pore in 1807, and reduced to a third-rate Power at, the peace of Tilsit, Prussia determined to make a noble effort at regeneration which would enable it once more to take its position among the leading nations of the world.

It began by breaking the tyrannical fetters of feudalism; it cast off the medieval incubus, restored the people to their rights, and thus by the infusion of new blood – the blood of free men into the nation – restored its vigour.

1 Try to make war if you can!! Nov 2nd, 1870. What about the bombardment of Paris? HAO.

In spite of the violent opposition of the privileged classes, the nation quietly and sternly pursued its course. Years flew by, and at last its efforts were crowned with success, and it reaped a glorious reward in the Campaigns of 1866.

If, instead of restoring the people to their rights according to the advice of "le nommé Stein,"[2] the ruling power had kept to the old feudal system; the Prussian musketeer, now a great fact, would have been impossible, because the material would have been wanting.

Let any one contrast the miserable state of Prussia immediately after the peace of Tilsit, with its apparition as a first-rate Power in 1866.

The object of the present treatise is to examine the glorious Campaign of 1866, in which the breech-loader, a new element of warfare, was for the first time introduced.

To give an idea of the power of this new instrument, it is only necessary to cite one example – the repulse of the Austrian attack in column at Chlum.

The column, 20,000 strong, advanced in the most perfect order to the attack. In twenty minutes, under the fire of the Prussian breech-loader, it lost 279 officers, 10,000 men, and 23 guns!

Now as no troops, however good, can possibly stand under such a fire as this, the grand question is, what we should do in England, in order to meet this new condition of warfare.

Perhaps the study of this pamphlet may give us some aid in arriving at a conclusion, and should that be the case, we shall be much indebted to its author, and the work of the translator will not have been in vain.

Henry Aimé Ouvry
Colonel, (Late 9th Lancers)
2, Bryanston Street, Portman Square, 18th January, 1870

Preface to the Second Edition

The translator little thought that the questions mooted in this pamphlet would be so soon put to the test when he issued it in January last; he begs to refer his readers to Chapter 7.

> In the next war that side will gain an unconditional, tactical preponderance, which best knows how to make use of its artillery, or rather that side which does not put off this practice till the moment of the commencement of the war, that is, the side whose artillery has had the best tactical training.

There is a great deal of talk about Army reform nowadays, but what we want immediately is Artillery, the rest can wait.

H.A. Ouvry
2, Bryanston Street, Portman Square,
Oct 13th, 1870

2 Napoleon ordered "le nommé Stein" to be arrested and sent out of Prussia.

Preface to the Third Edition

This work has now gone to a third edition, which speaks volumes in favour of the increased interest taken by the British officer in his profession.

The Author of this remarkable work is now known to be a Prussian captain named May; he fell gloriously in one of the late actions, but he has left his footsteps on the sands of military organization and tactics, and though dead he still speaketh; and if he could instil a little of the good sense and sound reasoning which is to be found in this work into the minds of those in power in this country, it would be well for us.

Looking at the manner in which our Army is recruited, and the style of recruits we obtain, I feel very uncertain as to whether the large sums of money we are about to spend in our reorganization will not be thrown away.

I have always been of opinion that there was but one way to form an army according to the requirements of the present day, and that is the Prussian system.

But we are told that this is impracticable, as Englishmen cannot be taken from their employments without positive ruin, and that they would never submit to compulsory service.

Perhaps they would not now; and the reason is sufficiently obvious – there is no proper element in England to meet the demand for recruits. The English people are divorced from the soil.

What we want is a reform á la Stein, and then we should be able to work the Prussian system with effect, and be able to produce armies of a material which would always chain victory to their colours, like the Romans of old; of which nation an illustrious historian has observed—

> In der Beherrschung der Erde liegt die Kraft des Mannes und des Staates: die Grösse Roms ist gebaut auf die ausgedehnteste und unmittelbarste Herrschaft der Bürger über den Boden und auf die geschlossene Einheit dieser also festgegründeten Bauerschaftt.

> In the command of the land lies the power of the individual and of the State: the greatness of Rome was founded on the most extended and immediate rule of the citizens over the land and soil, and on the absolute unity of a peasantry thus firmly planted on the same.

HAO

GENERAL MAP 1866. MAP 2

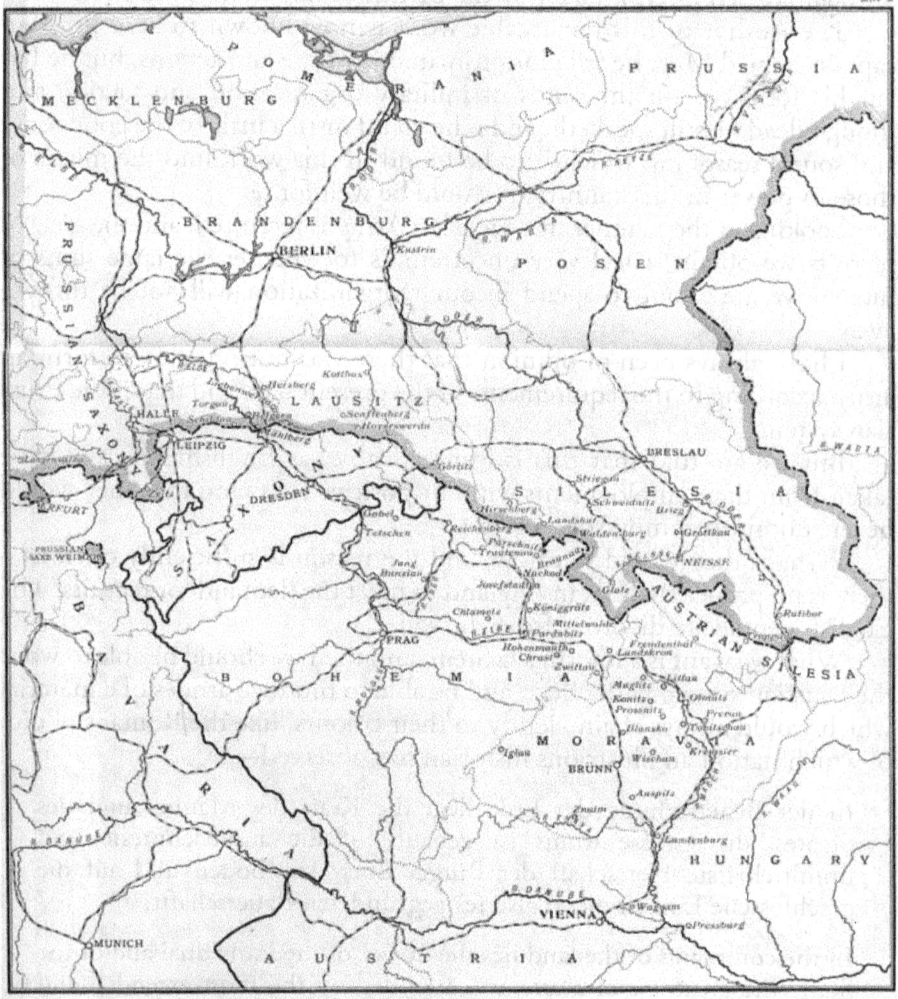

PRUSSIAN FRONTIER — English Miles — SAXON & BAVARIAN FRONTIERS

1

Introduction

The flood of pamphlets which have been published concerning tactical relations, since 1866, is already very significant. Should another now be added to the list, the author may allege that he takes that course because, in his opinion, none of those which have preceded him have made even a commencement towards a clear understanding of the rich experiences of 1866. Since all the wisdom of the system-mongers has been put an end to at one blow by hard facts, we should naturally expect to see any observations supported and grounded on the actual events. Between the description of a battle as it really is, or as a creative genius may please to represent it, there is indeed an immeasurable difference. Before the last campaigns, men were obliged to form strategical conclusions at second hand. The official accounts of military transactions from 1813–15, coloured by the distorting medium of many years, corresponded very little with the reality. These, assisted by the fantastical French accounts, formed the only materials to fill up a war picture, except, perhaps, a little aid drawn from the illusions and speculations of peacetime. Now, however, we have seen – seen with our own bodily eyes – the reality; and from this time forth, no one, however high his intellectual gifts, will be justified in judging concerning the "how" of the battle, or the tactics pursued, unless he should himself have witnessed this "how". He who has not been favoured by fortune in being permitted to take a part in these events may rail at his destiny, but he certainly can have no right or pretence to give an independent judgment with regard to tactics. The unnatural craving to judge of a world in which we have never lived is sure to be immediately rebuked; for we see at the first glance that the numerous essays, the substance of which the author often makes unfortunate attempts to bolster up on his own authority, are of his own invention, and of no value whatever.

Unfortunate in a like manner, also, appear to be the endeavours, now that the fresh life of experience is before our eyes, to attain to practical results by constructive philosophical reasoning from man's nature. However cleverly and logically we may try to develop the one out of the other, and finally to arrive at irrefragable conclusions by such reasoning, still, between a man thus constructed according to rule, and a Prussian musketeer, there will always be a wide difference. In order to form a correct judgment, it is necessary to have seen the man. All such philosophical deductions can have little value; they may possibly bear fruit for science and after ages, but are of little use for the present time, or for practical guidance.

We therefore take our stand here in the regions of real life and experience, but are far from believing that on that account alone we shall be enabled to produce anything of greater value than our above-mentioned predecessors. In the results which so quickly follow stirring events it is not easy to pick out the useful points. It is, perhaps, even more difficult than to speculate theoretically, seeing that real life leads as easily to error as to enlightenment. But, taking the view that it is our duty to publish the results of what we believe to be true, so that all may profit by it, we proceed; for even if our conclusions should be rejected by the tribunal of public opinion, scarcely anything will have been lost. All things will proceed in the path of progress, and we alone shall remain to be pitied, inasmuch as we shall have failed in our hopes of benefiting the community, and our vanity will suffer from the failure; but a straightforward honesty of intention will soon live that down (verschmerzen).

We are far from desiring, in the following pages, to introduce any startling novelties; such is not our object. If what we have to say be correct, many others must also at the same time have discerned and recognised it. However generally and simultaneously the conviction may prevail of the necessity of a tactical reform, it must be very apparent that all such innovations, before they are reduced to rule, must undergo a long course of probation by all descriptions of troops; must be introduced, then prohibited, and again reintroduced. This course will naturally prevail before judicious conclusions can be arrived at. With us Prussians the problem will meet its solution by the experiences of the late campaign, without any exterior aid. If then, these experiences are acknowledged to be sound, they must have an influence on the time and mode of carrying through the reforms in question. The experiences also of 1792–95 caused improvements in this direction, although at the expense of a very bitter lesson. It is the task of theory to anticipate and lend a hand in the development of these reforms. It can collect that which is loose and straggling, direct observation to the weightiest points, and excite discussion. The author, as well as the critic of any treatise on the subject, however honestly it may be written (and on that account above any petty vanity), feels that there can be no other criticism for it than the result. If the points treated on should be verified in the course of time, when a war may break out, or during its continuance, then the treatise is justified. If this should not be the case, it is condemned. A criticism which frequently allows itself to be blinded by mere finely-turned periods, and a critic who has not witnessed what is here spoken of, is not in a position to judge of it.

One condition, however, is indispensable, if we are to be of any service: we must have the courage of truth; we must represent things as they are, and not hide them under the meretricious cloak of a lying, so-called patriotic sentiment, concealing, praising, and euphemising, deceiving ourselves and others. We are men, and have fought manfully, so also have we erred; and we are sufficiently strong to hear the truth.

If hereafter we enunciate views or make propositions, it does not follow that they will be of general application; they are rather, purely founded on the state of the Prussian army, and what happened to it in the year 1866. They will have been elicited, not by the arm, but by the bearer of it.

2

General characteristics of the battle, founded on the results of 1866, and proof of the necessity and judiciousness of that mode of fighting

When we reflect on the battles of 1866 in order to consider them from a general point of view, we observe throughout one pervading phenomenon; that is, a most extraordinary extension of front with a very small degree of depth. The whole force appears extended in long thin lines, or separated into individual bodies fighting independently; above all, appears an inclination to surround the enemy by means of long extensions of the wings; and in this the preservation of the original "ordre de bataille" is quite out of the question. The different divisions of the army mix themselves up, or become mixed together, sometimes in the course of the battle, and sometimes before it becomes general. The several bodies of troops are formed on principles of the most different kinds; in action almost always in company columns, sometimes however in half battalions. The tactics of these company columns consist in throwing out swarms of skirmishers, their supports from time to time resolving themselves into the satire; the whole of the front line now bears some likeness to the confused attack of a horde of irregular cavalry, the impulse of each individual leader carrying with him that which he finds at his side. The second line of the army, which was in the rear, strives to cone up as quickly as possible to the front, in order to take part in the battle, and also because a considerable portion of the shot and shell intended for the first line passes over its head and falls into their ranks. But these in their close columns cannot so easily find cover on the field, and are obliged to bide their time, and by such delay become exposed to the feverish suspense which is unavoidable when troops are kept long under fire, and thus prevented from forgetting the danger, in the excitement of the struggle.

No wonder then, that officers and men eagerly seize on the first opportunity that offers, and make it a plea for pressing forward to the first line; the separate divisions push in whenever they can find room. By preference they incline towards the flanks, for there they can find the least impediment to their advance. Very often no reserve at all remains, or that which remains in the rear is too weak to answer the purposes of one.

It would be a great mistake to put into the category of errors, without any reservation, these individual and apparently irregular proceedings. Seeing that we have here to do with new phenomena, consequent on new conditions, these must be enquired into, and that which is found right and lawful in them acknowledged.

When the needle gun, at the commencement of the fifth year of its existence, was first generally issued to the troops, it was a standing order, insisted on by Generals who preached at all inspections and parades, "Gentlemen, throw out very few skirmishers – only one section, that is now as efficient as an old subdivision, let all the rest be kept well in hand." Experience, however, soon showed that the exact reverse of these theoretical rules, which appeared so judicious at the time, was the right practice. Above all things, every one sought to give full effect to the efficiency of his trustworthy arm. Why should they be held back? Why not strike with the full weight of the weapon in their possession? Thus they all dissolved themselves into a swarm of skirmishers, because in that formation the breech-loader can be best used, and was besides sufficiently analogous to a company column, which often stood more than ten deep, and fired from all possible positions. And this would take place, not so much at the word of command of their leader, who perhaps could only hear himself from the deafening noise of the guns and small arms, as from a natural consequence of the circumstances in which they were placed. We may now cast aside the imagination that the leader stands in the chivalric position laid down in the regulations for reviews and inspections, "one pace in front of the firing party to windward, in order calmly to direct the fire, to indicate the object to aim at, and to fix on the proper moment after a volley, at the command 'battalion forward,' to rush to the attack." This is a pretty "peacetime" picture, necessary for the purpose of training and instruction; even the apparently novel irregularity above alluded to must finally be reduced to fixed rules, otherwise exercises and instruction will be impossible.

The leader in battle, even the coolest and bravest, will be enabled, under cover of a tree or earthwork, with his glass at his eye, to superintend operations under fire much more carefully; a useless exposure of his person would be a mere act of vain bravado; an officer commanding troops has something better to do than to throw away his life to no purpose. A particular reason can alone justify his exposure to fire; such as, for the encouragement of his men, should they show an inclination to hang back, when he may place himself outside cover with assumed indifference; or if it should be the first time of his being under fire, he might expose himself for some minutes, in order to ascertain the effect of the whizzing of the bullets on his nervous system. His essential influence under these circumstances is bounded by some such short word of command as "Battalion take ground to the right 500 paces," if he should observe a better position; or if he should consider the moment favourable for an attack, he will simply say, "now, forward, march, hurrah!" and then rush on. If the troops are lying down, they arise just as they are; perhaps some of the men, becoming wild, think it their duty to commence firing in the direction of the enemy, their bullets whiz past the ears of their commander, who is in front, and then the whole rout (tross) rush after him to the attack. Some there are, who are of opinion that discretion is the better part of valour, and that it is better not to throw dirty water away till they have got clean; such hold back till those who have gone before have carried the position, when they follow with loud shouts on their traces.

This confused and irregular mode of attack should not be condemned as faulty; on the contrary, it is a necessary result of the new arm, and the peculiar training of the men. The great and zealous care with which from year to year we mark, verify, and note down each shot at musketry instruction, and the virtuous indignation with which every miss is put to the wrong side of the account by the instructor, becomes paid with interest. We should bring as many men as possible into the condition of being able to use their arm according to their own judgment.

This mode of fighting has an invariable result; the original depth of the order of battle, which consisted of a support behind the skirmishers, and a reserve behind these, is now superseded by a greater extension of the front line.

The far and sure-carrying arms of precision of the present time forbid supports and reserves in closed columns, except where the ground is favourable for such formations. It is apparent that either the old secondary formations have become impossible on account of the greater range of the missiles, which occasions the distance to become so much increased that there can finally be no relation between the supports and the engaged line; or the supports see in the loose, opened-out formation the proper means to adopt, and thus, of their own accord, they rush up at the double into the first line. With regard to this point of view, it would be well to study all the battles of 1866; it will be found that nearly all the companies of the second line soon forced themselves to the front. The mass of companies forces the line to extend laterally, as every newly-arriving body has a tendency to join itself on at the wings.

In this striving of the supports and reserves to force themselves forward into the fighting line lies the impossibility of preserving the old-fashioned order of battle, or even the primitive tactical formation.

Every division in the rear which has hitherto remained in close column rushes in where necessity or a possibility shows itself. An interchange between the engaged line and its supports is evidently impossible; there is not even the smallest guarantee that a company will fight together with the skirmishers which it has itself thrown out, or that the companies of a battalion, or the battalions of a regiment, will ever come together. Let any one compare the state of every single battle of 1866, with regard to the positions of every division of the army after the troops had been well engaged, and the old-fashioned order of battle. It would however be very rash to conclude that all this was a great series of error; far better would it be to ascertain how far these new phenomena are legitimate and reasonable.

The mounted officers are obliged to dismount, which makes the supervision and direction impossible, which is so easy in peace-time manœuvres. Frequently the dismounted staff officer, somewhat unaccustomed to quick marching over stock and stone, is scarcely able to keep up with his battalion; thus the breaking up into columns of companies is for him a solution of his difficulty. He thinks that certainly the four officers commanding the companies will know what to do, so he attaches himself to a company. The original officers of lines are in the same predicament; their lines are broken up and scattered in all parts of the battle; thus they are obliged to give up all idea of commanding them, and attach themselves to the first company of infantry that offers, and, in order to do something, command that. It thus happens that some companies, favoured by chance, have besides their own captain, a major, a colonel, and a general as well; the company will not, perhaps be better commanded, but those officers will at least have done all that remained in their power. They are all in the front line, and by their personal example influence those among whom they have placed themselves, but in fact they have become mere captains of companies; the whole line of battle has thus become nothing more than a fight between a number of company leaders and the opposing enemy.

This manner of exclusively fighting by columns of companies, and their employment on all occasions, is a momentum which has peculiarly developed itself in the Prussian army. For this reason our (Prussian) captains are relatively the most precious portion of the whole army.

Our company leaders are, on an average, from 30 to 40 years old, an age in which the body is obedient to all the demands of the will; and this will, after it has conquered all the immaturity of youth, still possesses sufficient elasticity to work actively as well as zealously. The high sense of duty, and the perfect knowledge of all the forms of the service, which have not yet struck root in the immature minds of the younger officers, necessarily affords the company leader the opportunity of possessing the first requisite in warlike events, viz the fullest command over all his subordinates. The constant petty annoyances of peace-service have not yet disgusted him, and rendered him listless (mürbe). A campaign still appears to him an end of the annoyance of being obliged to look after and keep in order the equipments of the fourth part of a battalion, and the everyday details of the service. He sees a future still before him, and ambition – that grand lever in all warlike affairs – is still lively in him. The fainthearted man will be carried away, and hurried forward by his active comrade who fights by his side. Thus, the company leader sets an example which cannot be surpassed. Should he fall, the senior lieutenant steps into his place; he has long been waiting with eagerness for the moment when, with no one above him, he will have nothing to attend to but the enemy.

Many a fight is thus won by the company leaders. The preference, however, here given to one rank is not intended as a reproach to the rest. We are all men, and act according to our nature. Youth is always bold, reckless, thinking only of the present moment; age, on the contrary, is prudent and egotistical; it is only in exceptional dispositions that these two advantages are developed in the same individual. These are the few who govern the world, and are honoured as heroes by the present age, and by posterity. The same company leader who, at thirty years of age, distinguished himself at the head of his company, at forty becomes a field officer; but ten years of grinding service, including continual inspections, has corroded his freshness, unless he is endowed by nature with an iron constitution. He has now become listless; he has got children and the rheumatism; the bold, active spirit has fled; he is therefore no longer fitted to show a personal example in his position to those about him. Requirements will be made which his calm judgment will often not approve of. He now begins to reckon up the amount of his pension, and to consider whether his conduct has been such as will recommend him for further promotion, or whether, with a possible failure in prospect, it would not be better for him to get out of the way in time. He looks on war without any illusions. The wet bivouac, the never-ending hardships, the inability the day after the battle even to hunt up more than one cigar in the midst of a quarter of a million of men, are most lively reminiscences with him. He becomes contented with his present condition, and looks for nothing more in the future. Should he go again into the field, he is led there by honour and duty, not by ambition. Ambition inspires individuals to wish to do more than others – more than is or can be ordered. Honour bids them do their duty. It is, however, only the ambitious officer who does that which is uncommon – that is to say, who achieves greatness; and let it be reiterated that it is of great moment to preserve ambition and to fresh elasticity of spirit up to old age.

It is only an iron nature which can bear up against gnawing cares, and by a self-dependent faith still preserve its belief in a future. It is, however, impossible: to apply this ideal rule to the generality of men. These listless characters have, for the most part, put themselves out of the way of becoming Generals. Those who still continue to serve are men who, from external circumstances, have passed through the several ranks easily, and who bring to the office of General the whole of their mental powers, unweakened as they have received them from nature, or else they are of the sort that have had reliance in themselves and made their own way. These last are those who possess united the impulse of youth and capability to see things from an enlarged point of view. On them rests the hope of the army.

It is then naturally indicated that we should bring up our companies independently against the enemy, in order to utilize the full powers of our army. As many company leaders as there are in the fighting line of battle, so many individual wills are there which we may rely on are filled with the one idea of acting against the enemy with the greatest vigour, and which possess most perfectly the means of carrying their ideas into execution.

The material of our (Prussian) men favours these tactics in a high degree. The North German soldier is generally somewhat dull and quiet, of sound though not great natural intellect, and without personal ambition. Fair words have no effect on him; there is only one thing that makes any impression, that is – the deed (die That). When he finds himself suddenly encompassed by the dangers of war, he desires to have some one at hand to give him confidence that all is going on well. His eye naturally turns to his officer. If he sees in the calm look of his commander that he must be obeyed here the same as in peace-time, if he sees him go forward undismayed, he generally asks for nothing more. An example pleases, inspires, and overawes him. He has an admirable quality, which only wants to be developed, and that is, the desire heartily to admire some one; and he blindly follows his leader with unbounded attachment to his person.

The best foundation for the authority of an officer over his subordinates lies in attaching them to himself personally by his actions, without seeking it, perhaps even while seeming to avoid it.

Trite attachment to the person of his officer, far more than ambition and patriotism, is generally the motive which inspires the soldier to the utmost. If he should have overcome the first novelty of the situation, and have got confidence in himself, all his good qualities may be developed to the full extent. His naturally quiet disposition does not induce him to rush on impetuously, but rather to go thoroughly to work. Like a true German, who always clings with a religious tenacity to his property, he now concentrates all his affection on his weapon, which gave him many a weary hour in peace-time. So long as the danger is indefinite, he feels himself uncomfortable; but when he sees it before him he soon collects himself: and when at last he stands face to face with the enemy; he remembers with a certain satisfaction many a Sunday affray, and considers that he is now bound to improve the occasion, which this time certainly will not bring his name into the defaulters' book. We (Prussians) can, without too much risk, venture on a greater division and intermixture of our companies. In most cases the soldier, if he has once formed an attachment to the person of his officer, will take pains to find him again; and thus we are enabled to permit of his fighting separately with confidence. On an average our (Prussian) soldier compared with the soldiers of other continental armies, is of a physical strength which instils a certain confidence.

The reverse of the character of our soldiers, which consists in a want of personal ambition, and the necessity for the immediate supervision of their officers, will be reserved for a later consideration.

Should foreign armies think of imitating our company-column fights, they must take into consideration how it stands with them with regard to the fundamental principle; that is, the relations between their officers and men. They will otherwise adopt the disadvantages without gaining the benefit.

There lies also in the great defensive power of our arm, an element which renders these narrow irregular lines more capable of resistance than is apparent at a first view. They will always be able to repulse feeble attacks; even the smallest detachments will not allow themselves to be demolished without ceremony.

It must be most distinctly understood, that these loose irregular formations, which we have here alluded to are not to hold good on all occasions and in all circumstances. So long as an officer believes himself to be in a position to gain the same results by keeping to the systematic forms of the service, he is quite right to do so, but let him recollect that one, atom too much of this is pernicious. Let officers look to the spirit of these apparently irregular formations, and not allow themselves to be taken by surprise or be disconcerted should they manifest themselves. An army which cannot venture to trust in the individual worth of its soldiers, so far as to let them fight in this manner, cannot reckon on the advantages to be derived from the operation of the breech-loader.

3

Necessity of a counterpoise against the dissolving action of the battle

In the foregoing chapters we have sought to lay down how the loose and apparently irregular formation of our fighting line is a necessary consequence of the peculiarity, of our army, and that it is attended with very beneficial results. It must, however, never be forgotten, that here, where the strength of our army lies, is also to be found its most sensible weakness. The more the different parts of the army have a disposition to fight separately, the greater will be the strength of hand required to hold them together, and arrange matters so that all their unchained power, instead of following their own ideas eccentrically and without plan, shall finally work towards a point fixed upon by the eye of their commander. A mere mechanical leading will produce no result, because the leader would then not understand how to use his precious instrument; a faulty leading is still worse, for it would ruin it.

This loose individual mode of combatting requires a counterpoise which must be twofold. The first and most important is the Commander-in-Chief, who remains on horseback out of the range of fire; he watches over, and has by him a strong reserve to reinforce the front line when necessary. The other counterpoise is the officer commanding the front line, whose essential duty it is to execute all necessary movements in the same.

We will speak now of this latter point. The greatest danger to this line is, that the enemy, by an attacking force concentrated on one point, and suddenly applied, may break it, and drive back these small individual divisions which are fighting without any plan. Trautenau and Langensalza afford proof of this.

The fighting line cannot always receive benefit from a reserve which stands intact in the rear; the blow comes so suddenly that the reserve hurrying up to its support, only comes partially into the fight, and is wholly enveloped in the mass of the retiring line. This being so, the fighting line should seek a resource in itself, to resist such an attack effectually.

For this purpose it is necessary that the superior officer in the front line should form into close columns all who are not actually required as skirmishers, and place them in such positions as may appear good to him according to the nature of the ground, and where they will be most useful without any regard as to whether they happen to be before or behind the line of fire. But in these formations all idea of the original ones, whether of companies or battalions, should be laid aside. There are often on one spot hundreds of men, of all sorts of troops, mixed up together. Instead of forming a half battalion in close columns of these, without reference to their original belongings, why should recourse be had to a formation of a number of small troops and trooplets (Trüpchen) according to their original belongings, which would have no effectual power of resistance, and which would, for the most part, dissolve again in a moment?

Our (Prussian) army has an advantage which cannot be too much appreciated, in the general uniformity of its component parts. There is no reason why a body thus formed provisionally from men belonging to different regiments, should be at all inferior to one formed regularly according to their original belongings; this is an advantage which must be utilized. If it can possibly be done without disadvantage, certainly the original connection of the formation of the troops must be preserved. A first aid towards this is the formation of an order of battle conformable to the purpose, that is, to send in the same direction all the men of the same corps; thus, at least, their intermixture is only possible to a certain degree.

Up to this time we have held the peacetime view that a regiment was not a tactical, but merely an administrative unity; tactical units being battalions and brigades. The campaign, however, soon taught us a different lesson. Whoever has had a number on his shoulder will know the importance of a man coming in astray from his division, seeing the number of his regiment on a shoulder-strap, even if it should be on that of a dead man; he is like one who, after long wanderings, suddenly finds that he has returned and found his home.

There should be no great difference in uniform. When a man passes a regiment, his eye involuntarily turns to the little mark on the shoulder; he sees nothing but that. Regiments especially are the most marked tactical units. If we would, in the necessary intermingling of a fight, collect and reassemble the troops in the easiest manner possible, the different regiments must be kept together. When a regiment goes entire into action, not only is the ambition of the individual active, but also that of the whole regiment which fights for its renown.

The homogeneity of a regiment[1] does not suffer from the mixing together of the most different elements, if they are all of the same value. But for this reason it is necessary to make no difference between Fusilier battalions and others. The very small advantage that can ever accrue from having any kinds of picked battalions, is far outweighed by the very grave disadvantage of having in our army some battalions that are worse than others. In the equality of all parts of our army, and of all its officers, lies its most powerful impulse, its strength, and its essential superiority over all other armies. The idea that these picked battalions are intended for a particular service may be

1 Note: 4 companies = 1 battalion; 3 battalions = 1 regiment.

dismissed as an illusion. A battle is capable, at any moment, of assuming all kinds of phases, consequently an infantry is required which can be utilized in all cases.

If the superior officer, who commands the first line, wishes to fulfil his duty properly in his sphere of action, he must direct the whole chaos of the surrounding fight. But, in this chaos, parts of the troops originally under his command become mixed up in the most varied manner with others. If he should only command his own part, the force of the rest would not be utilized. No officer would willingly encroach on the rights of another leader, but it is most especially necessary that every leader should have the right, unconditionally, to dispose of all the troops that happen to be in his vicinity. The senior officer commands, and posts the companies or the battalions together, according to his judgment. He assembles together, in strong masses, all that are within his reach at the spot where he foresees an attack, after which the columns can be deployed, and again resume the offensive.

Thus a strong resource is always to be found in the front line, weak as it may appear to be, if there should be a leader at the decisive point who knows how to command, and thinks of nothing but the tactical emergency.

But it may be objected that such tactics would make it very difficult, after the battle, to reassemble the troops thus mingled together, in their proper corps and divisions. To this we may reply, consider the case of the battle of Charbusitz, where three different armies lead mutually to pick out their own men.

And, again, it may be remarked – first gain your battle, that is the chief point, then it will be far easier to disentangle and collect your men into their proper places, than after it is lost. If, therefore, the victory can be gained by this free disposal of men of different corps and divisions, it can not only be justified, but should be enjoined.

Further, it may possibly be objected that collisions will, under such circumstances, unavoidably occur between the several leaders of corps and divisions. To this it may be answered, that most certainly such a disposal of men à discrétion is only possible when the officers of all ranks, without exception, are educated in the highest degree, both in an intellectual and military point of view, and are in a position to rely on their own tact for the solution of difficult and weighty points, rather than on any prescribed scheme of tactics.

One single individual who is destitute of the above qualifications, has the power of causing the most ruinous consequences, which is a fresh proof of the great advantages to be gained by having all officers formed on one principle.

This formation of scattered elements in a moment must become one of the most precious movements to employ in every battle, but the right moment must be seized, as the opportunity, not being taken advantage of, may never return.

This absolute right of disposal of men of other corps and troops, may be regarded from another and most important point of view, and that is, the nature of our soldiers, which we must here again take into consideration.

He who considers that our men are all heroes because they are derived from a brave class is very considerably mistaken. If only all soldiers, of their own accord, would simply do their duty in battle, an army would be perfectly invincible, and would not require any tactical instruction whatever.

But man has in his composition a natural desire of self-preservation, an egotism and indolence united with many sensual desires, but at the same time also germs, which are capable of being developed into higher qualities. He who has come to a consciousness of this, not only knows it, he breathes and feels with his whole soul that there are spiritual powers of a higher nature, which stand opposed to the sensual bias, and that he must combat this with all his might; it cannot; however be done without a struggle. Who would ever maintain that death was indifferent to him? for in the tumult of the battle danger is not so much despised as forgotten or ignored. The less the powers of the mind have attained to this freedom of development of its spiritual powers, so much the more will the senses hold sway. The man of the people who is accustomed to rough or dangerous work has rather deadened his sense by custom, than conquered it.

The greater number of the men go bravely into the fight because their common sense tells them that it must be so, that it would be shameful to sneak off; if they cannot do so with a good grace, they make the best of a bad bargain.

So long as the soldier knows that the eye of his officer is upon him, he instinctively feels the inspiration and willingly bows to it. But in the supreme moment, in which danger and death are imminent, suddenly this accustomed link is broken, the eye of his leader is directed towards the enemy in the front, the troops hurry towards the fire and among the hissing cannon shot; the man sees death in his front, and a nice road-side ditch by his side; it is the temptation to a theft, he sneaks quickly into it, and his company is soon far away from him. Those who immediately follow take him for a wounded man. Presently he stands up, he has become a "straggler"; no one interrogates him, the only one who has a right to do so is in front. Perhaps he now seeks to make himself useful, in a safe place, by helping to get the wounded or prisoners to the rear, or he turns simply to marauding. Opportunity makes the thief.

This sneaking off in all kinds of ways is by no means a rare occurrence. It is chiefly by these kinds of stragglers that such a serious melting away of many companies in battle is caused. The next morning, when the hot coffee appears, by a most remarkable instinct, they all happen to have found their places again. The same man, who, while overlooked, bears himself bravely, will fall off when left to himself. And let us here be very frank. Is not this phenomenon so very natural to man, that in a modified manner it prevails universally? The officer who feels that the eye of a General whom he fears is upon him, does wonders; but if the same officer should be isolated and left to himself, the strained nerves slacken, all the bodily and mental instincts reassume their empire, and thus he does his duty and nothing more. Why are leaders immediately blamed if whole bodies of troops do not behave well? Because every one feels that troops never behave ill so long as there is a ruling spirit to inspire them.

From this then we may conclude that the watching over troops is a necessity. It is not sufficient that the eye of the leader is directed to the enemy; to advance and leave half the men behind on the way cannot lead to any advantage. The company should have an officer in the supernumerary rank, who should be responsible on his honour that he will keep there, and not rush to seek his laurels in the front. Then it will be easy to bring the company full and complete into action.

4

Fixed regulations and their modification

In order practically to carry out all that has been spoken of in the preceding chapters, no innovations on the established regulations are necessary, as these generally act like a double-edged sword that cuts both ways. To change that which has become customary and deeply rooted in an army is always a critical matter, but to make wholesale alterations is ruinous. When all old rules are suddenly altered no one knows where to turn, and for fear of making a false move everything remains at a standstill. The latitude given in our regulations concerning the company columns is so broad, that it is only necessary to stretch a point when an emergency requires it, in order to meet any case that may arise; and after the object has been accomplished, the line can then be drawn in sharper again.

Let it be considered to what confusion it would lead if every one thought himself bound to invent new formations for particular cases, in which the regulations seemed to be unsuited. The following will exemplify this. The officer commanding a battalion had an idea that he could substitute a formation of his own for that laid down in the regulations for a battalion marching on a chaussée in columns of sections, if it were to be surprised by cavalry. He considered that his idea was too good to be thrown away, and held that at the words "Column, form!" the men were to open out right and left, and get into the ditch on each side of the chaussée and prepare to fire upwards. He thought that the cavalry would run the gauntlet between his two lines, and that not one of them would escape. But in what degree these ditches would protect the men, or if the enemy's cavalry were to attack their long thin lines from the other side, remained questions not comprised in his calculations. The manœuvre, however, was frequently practised, and the men who were accustomed at the well-known word of command to close up into serried ranks, and show a front on all sides, were now suddenly, entirely of their own accord, and at the same word of command, to open out, get into a ditch, and then face inwards! Very fortunately the battalion did not happen to meet with any cavalry. But this proves to what it would lead, if every exception were to be tortured into a rule, and if individuals were to think themselves justified and in duty bound to correct the faults of a whole system.

There is, however, one point in which we could wish that a departure might be made from the standing regulations. We refer to an uninterrupted and direct interchange between the line of skirmishers and their supports. According to the regulations, both the line of skirmishers and their supports are under one command. Now, it may he gathered from the foregoing remarks that this connection is not at all certain of being maintained; for while many companies are engaged, every single company is broken up, and the different subdivisions skirmishing in front are under a divided command, and have no firm, closed support in their rear, which is so essentially necessary. The leaders have to look after so many different things, that they can hardly accomplish anything in any direction. This dependence of one part of a company on another should be abolished. Whole companies should be employed together as skirmishers, and whole companies should remain closed up as supports; thus each leader will know what he has to do. The reciprocal action of the supports and the skirmishers can only be prescribed by the enemy. The leaders of both companies will have their eyes directed towards the opposing force, and can act as the opportunity presents itself.

5

Influence of the General Commanding-in-Chief, and of the reserve on the battle

But, however careful may be the leading in the front line of the contending army, its supports and reserves included, it will never be in a position to repulse effectually an energetic attack by the enemy directed on one point. It is a law incontrovertible, that troops which have become slack from continued fighting (vom gefecht mürbe gemachter Truppen) are never capable of resisting the assault of a fresh and vigorous force. The enemy who is well acquainted with the advantages appertaining to the initiative will take care to strike the blow suddenly, and with overwhelming numbers, and not allow the distant reserve time to come up. If there should be no fresh reserve in the rear, then most certainly the attack cannot be repulsed.

The exclusive guarantee, and indeed the first condition, of the victorious result of a battle is a strong reserve, directly at the disposition of the General commanding. We do not mean one battalion, one squadron, and one battery, or what was up to this time commonly designated "a special reserve," to be kept in the rear, but rather one quarter or one third of the whole force. This reserve should not be posted for the purpose of occasionally coming to the front, in order to give a momentary preponderance at any particular point, or to take advantage of an unfavourable eventuality; but it should rather serve as a firm repli to the front line when it has no longer the power to resist, or is broken through by a decisive attack of the enemy, and should form a firm mass, untouched by the disturbing tumult of the battle, behind which the retreating line might be able to rally and reform, and against whose flesh and well-formed columns, drawn up in the most perfect defensive order, the force of the pursuing enemy would be broken. The reserves have essentially a defensive object – they should stand fast and guarantee the security of the lighting line.

But it may be objected to this, that in the solicitude to prevent an unfavourable issue, by standing on the defensive, the opportunity is lost of gaining the battle by means of an attack; that the first attack is thereby robbed of the forces which can alone render it successful; and that the history of wars is full of examples of the pernicious results of placing large reserves of troops which are thereby taken from the battle. To this we reply, that, in the individualized method of fighting which we consider necessary for our army, it is right to throw only as many troops into the direct dissolving chaos of battle as are strictly necessary. Battalions become swallowed up without any perceptible result. Three battalions which are fresh at the end of a battle for an attack, tend more to a decisive effect than six which have been fighting all day. By a wise retention, the strength of the troops is increased, while the enemy is perhaps induced to engage the whole of his power. He who has the last shilling in his pocket will conquer in the war, and he who has the last fresh battalion in hand will wine the battle. Let any officer who has ever been in a difficult position in a battle be asked which he would consider most advantageous for himself and the battle, to have a few more battalions in the chaos of the light, or to have a well-posted reserve of fresh troops to retire upon? It appears that in nearly all the battles of 1866 a great portion of the troops never came under fire at all; at Trautenau there were five battalions that it was not thought necessary to bring to the front, or indeed to use at all. But instead of keeping these troops closed up as a reserve on one spot, they were moved about from a kind of conscientious anxiety to give them something to do, and to enable them to contribute somewhat towards the result of the day. But it is often very apparent, that, they contribute in the greatest degree towards that end when they remain quietly in the rear, and that the troops engaged in the battle advance with greater boldness and confidence when they know that there is a strong reserve behind there; and thus we have a reserve which answers a double purpose.

A corps d'armée may be thus divided – fifteen battalions to fight in the first line, and ten to form the reserve. When the attack of the first line cannot penetrate further, and should its strength begin to flag, of course the enemy will take advantage of this failing, and will in its turn assume the offensive. If the fighting line, in spite of the advantage of the defensive – which has now gone over to them – cannot withstand the attack, they will by their retreat draw the pursuing enemy into the sphere of action of their reserve formation; this is intact, and further has the advantage of the defensive, and new chances may happen.

It is of little use to say that, in the endless combinations of a battle, it is not likely that this phase would manifest itself. Those who perceive in such a proposal something more than a mere pedantic school regulation, and see it in the light of a lively idea flowing from observation which, though always remaining the same, is still capable of being adapted in the most varied forms, under the most varied circumstances, will appreciate the true spirit of this view.

Compare the course of the battles of 1866, which are founded on facts. It is from a contemplation of these that this view has been formed. It is quite true that a weak, offensive movement on the part of the enemy can often be repulsed by the front line, but the contrary may also happen. Even if the intention should be to remain most strictly on the defensive, the same strong reserve can never be dispensed with. When the enemy cannot penetrate any further against the front, he will frequently move in long circuits in the rear, and on the flanks of the army which stands upon the defensive. Its reserves, posted in the rear, will meet these troops who are thus endeavouring to turn their flanks, and in such partial combats many situations may occur, if the troops are ably distributed, in which the side that was originally the weakest will, at certain points, become the strongest. Let anyone compare the battles of 1866.

It is only by these strong reserves that the General commanding can secure the means of exercising a perfect influence and mastery over the battle when it has once commenced. Should he neglect this, he simply leaves the result to chance. This, however, may not prevent the troops fighting in the front from possibly gaining a brilliant victory.

An order of battle can be drawn up in this manner: A first line, which may be formed according to the occasion and the nature of the ground, here in great swarms of skirmishers, there in close columns, either massed or in several lines, but having this in common – that at one and the same moment in the battle, all can immediately be engaged; and a strong reserve, undisturbed by the tumult of battle, in the rear. While the General commanding partially gives his attention to the first line, in which his essential influence consists in directing an adequate number of troops from the front on the decisive points (whose leading is the business of the subordinate officer), his eye watches over all, and he always makes the immediate dispositions with regard to the reserve.

This necessary independence of the first line is founded on an essential condition, viz that the two contending armies are armed with breech-loaders. Under the former state of things, a renewal of a repulsed attack could be reckoned on; now, it is impracticable. After a long and careful preparation by fire, the decisive movement comes as quick as lightning. Troops from rearward formations come up too late to be of any use, as the critical moment so soon passes away. To renew an attack on a defensive position, with any happy result, when its strength is once known, is quite out of the question.

But here the question first occurs: How will it be when there are breech-loaders on both sides? Will not all hitherto mentioned be considered as an accidental result of one campaign, in which only one side was so armed, and therefore leading to no general conclusions? Must we not seek elsewhere than in the battles of 1866 for proofs?

An examination of the battles of this campaign will tend to settle the point.

6

On the battles of 1866, with regard to the cooperation of the several branches of the Service

A most striking phenomenon is to be observed throughout all the battles of 1866. They were essentially begun, continued, and ended by the infantry. The other arms played a mere secondary part, and not infrequently their influence was unfelt. It is very easy to give reasons in each individual case, and to explain why, under the circumstances, it was found impossible to bring the other branches of the service into action, the common and principal reason being "we did not understand how, or consider it necessary, to make use of them, and therefore made no effort to bring them into action." This is scarcely a reproach. The army of 1866 was a "peacetime" army, as excellent as a long and careful peace-training could ever form. Its teachers were infantry soldiers, who only knew well their particular arm, and trusted implicitly to it. Thus, in the pressure to advance, so long as it seemed to succeed, there was a strong tendency to rely wholly on this convenient and ready instrument. The superiority of the infantry arm over that of the enemy, had the effect of rendering the inadequacy of the other branches of the service imperceptible, except in very rare cases. There was necessarily an absence of that calm coolness which war experience alone can give, and which instinctively informs the leader when the one branch of the troops should e aided by the others, and enables him to employ all at the proper moment. So the infantry rushed on, and when its advance was checked, in its impatience it extended to the right and left, till the whole again moved on. This manœouvre generally succeeded. The superiority of the arm justified the greater license.

But the triumph of one particular branch of the army is only possible at the expense of the others. In the sequel we will examine the duties of each branch in its turn, and will here merely refer to a few facts, in order to understand more clearly their mutual relations.

It is a remarkable circumstance that out of 113 guns taken on the field at Koniggrätz, 108 fell into the hands of the infantry, while the cavalry only took 5. Under the conditions of the contest, it was to have been expected that the cavalry would have made the capture; these conditions were – splendid cavalry ground, uncommon extension of the enemy's front, badly supported wings, and much demoralization and disunited tactics; and on our own side a more numerous cavalry. Certainly there will be no want of reasons to show us the causes of this failure of the cavalry. But all these reasons put together prove nothing more than that it was not understood, or not considered necessary, that they should act on the occasion. A similar example is afforded by the artillery at Koniggrätz; the first army, from 8 till 2 o'clock, carried on essentially an artillery action. But did their artillery attain its object? That could only be to make a breach in the enemy's formation, when the infantry could attack, and thus prepare their defeat. But they never once succeeded in making any impression on the imposing Austrian artillery formation; they barely succeeded in holding their own (ihrer Ilant zu wehren). Had not the Prussian infantry appeared in the rear of the Austrians artillery, they would have had no occasion to surrender their position. Thus, in this battle, the artillery was not capable of fulfilling its task. If it be objected that, on this occasion, the object of the artillery was not to decide matters, but merely to hold the enemy in check till the Second Army, or the Elbe Army should come into action, and that these remarks are made rashly, without due regard to the circumstances; we reply, that it was not only possible, but even probable, that these armies might have been met on the march by the Austrian reserves, and the time and place of the probable meeting should have been well considered. If, then, these armies had only been in a measure delayed by the Austrians, we should finally have been obliged to attack, if we meant to obtain any decisive results. Would the preparatory artillery fire have been sufficient for this attack?

It may perhaps also be said, that the Austrian artillery had the advantage of being on the defensive, and that always gives an advantage over the offensive; but there lies a contradiction in this the artillery of one side must always be on the defensive, but that it must therefore necessarily conquer, can hardly be maintained. It is the business, that is, the tactics of the one to make (if there is only room to place the guns) such dispositions as will take away the advantage of the defensive of the other. If the artillery concede, that under the circumstances they will not be able to effect their object, then all the work is thrown on the shoulders of the infantry.

The expression "infantry tactics" is essentially a scientific abstraction, necessary for the fixing of scientific ideas and elementary forms. In a battle there is no such thing as infantry tactics; tactics are for the handling of the three branches of the service united. It cannot be said at any moment during a battle – here the artillery tactics cease, and those of the infantry commence; both of them are constantly interwoven one with the other. Desperate circumstances can alone justify the employment of the infantry only, in the crisis of a battle; no theoretical rules can be laid down for infantry fighting under such circumstances, any more than for a battalion that is without its arms. Should the Generals commanding insist on the infantry fighting alone, they certainly would not know how to make use of their materials.

When the infantry blazes away at the enemy, and the enemy returns it; when the cavalry of both sides mutually attack, and the two artilleries cannonade each other, or, according to the technical expression, "when they mutually seek to draw the fire upon themselves," that tactics of the united arms can no longer be spoken of. Faults committed incur no penalty when both sides are equally blamable. The essential lever in war is the infantry; if that be broken, the battle is decided. Thus all the three branches should concentrate their force against the enemy's infantry, and only pay attention to the other arms in as far as it is absolutely necessary for the purpose of defence. It is a great truth that to work with concentrated force on one point – in battle as in the ordinary affairs of life – is always a warrant for success. The artillery, however good or numerous it may be, will never avert the loss of the battle, when once the infantry has been forced to give way.

This "secret" of victory is not one necessary to be kept; it may be known, and still the power to make use of it may not be possessed. This point is the test of the eminent warlike qualities in the leaders of armies. It is only when this is felt, and when instinctively, and without intermission, this one decisive mark is aimed at, without regard to any minor object, that the highest results can be attained.

7

On several propositions towards paralysing the action of the breech-loader

If neglect and failure with regard to the tactics of the three arms were less felt on account of the needle gun in 1866, in future the chance will not arise again; the question therefore is, what element is now necessary to secure a preponderance?

The proposals hitherto made are scarcely satisfactory; from one we may deduce, that the firing will be mutually left off, and that the bayonet will then again resume its old (?) rights. But that can only happen when both sides have come to an agreement to renounce all firing; otherwise the attacked party would always use the great defensive power of its weapon against the one attacking; and the fights of Nachod, Laufach, Tauberbischoffsheim show sufficiently what the result would be. Others put forward regimental artillery-mitrailleuses. It is not to be conceived how the quick movements of infantry on every kind of ground can be followed with instruments of this kind, or how they can be made use of under a fire of small arms. Only let the wood of Maslowed be recollected. What would the fourteen Prussian battalions have been able to do with such mitrailleuses? An arm that can only be reckoned on at times, is worse than none at all: it leads to false calculations. These artificially forced ideas (Treibhausideen) all come to nothing in the simple, mighty wave of battle.

The supposition that at the commencement of the next war we shall remain strictly on the defensive, and allow the enemy's columns to advance among our bullets is a very rational one. If only the enemy will do us this pleasure, the matter is soon settled. They will, however, think twice, and well digest the matter; and possibly restrain a little their fiery dispositions. They will, perhaps, forming conclusions from our rapid proceedings in 1866, think to make us rush in among their bullets, and when we have been well sickened, go in at us with the bayonet. Thus we may stand, fighting shy of each other, and if we should further develop the consequences of this picture, we may both seek to get out of the mess by manœuvring. But the matter would not take this same course.

In the next war that side will obtain an unconditional tactical preponderance which best knows how to make use of its artillery, or rather that side which does not put off this practice till the moment that the war commences, in fact the side whose artillery has had the best tactical training.

8

Influence of the Artillery in general, and its action in the Campaign of 1866

A position which is defended can only be approached to within 400 or 500 paces by troops covered by skirmishers. A preparatory fire of small arms against the defenders who are under cover will never have the effect of rendering a storm possible; according to the most simple calculation, the storming party, however strong its columns, will be repulsed, always supposing the position to be in the hands of brave troops.

But nothing can withstand a powerful preparatory attack by artillery; if the element to be broken be the infantry, it can only be done by this means. That in particular cases, the victory can be gained with an inferior artillery does not invalidate this rule. There are heads that can utilize the most deficient materials; genius, or an iron character in a General, creates characters in subordinates which would not otherwise be developed; many such became active in 1866, but they cannot be reckoned on as a rule.

As we have before remarked, we cannot boast much of the support we experienced from our artillery in the last war. If we examine the whole of the battles, we find that, in spite of the large number of the disposable batteries, our artillery was not often in a position to command the field in the presence of the Austrian guns. We brought a numerous and imposing artillery into the field, it is true, but how many guns overcame into action? they planted themselves here and there among the reserve, and never found place anywhere to engage. It would indeed be sufficiently amusing to hear this conduct excused; an artillery officer who has a tactical eye for the ground will always be able to find room. We will give an example.

At the battle of Trautenau suitable ground for artillery was wanting. In that long and sanguinary action, in which the Austrian artillery was never for a moment silent, very few Prussian batteries were brought into action, and these only very partially. Their continuance under fire may be judged of by the returns of the loss. The sixteen batteries had only seven wounded out of the whole loss of 1,338 men; of the total loss of seventy-eight horses, two only fell to the lot of the artillery; this makes not half a man a battery, and one-eighth of a horse.

Most certainly it was not from a want of personal courage in the artillery leaders, but the ground appeared questionable, and it was not considered prudent to expose the artillery even to the possibility of a loss; and for this reason the greater part of the batteries were not brought into the actual battlefield, and even the few who were engaged were withdrawn just at the moment when their activity was commencing; as if it were better to lose the battle than a single gun. There was neither time nor space wanting to have established the whole of the ninety-six guns. It is, however, only those leaders whose talent is able to command the tactical situation who can carry through a bold and daring enterprise. Artillerists without tactical training and daring, who have merely a knowledge of technical gunnery, will always find excuses and make impossibilities.

We will here adduce an example, taken it is true from a peacetime occurrence, but which is not on that account the less instructive with regard to judging of difficulties. At a divisional field-day a troop of horse-artillery was retiring at a gallop, it came to a ditch, it pulled up, took ground to the right, and passel the ditch by a bridge some hundred paces farther on; at the same time and place, and under the same circumstances, a field battery of twelve-pounders came at a gallop to the same ditch, without hesitating a moment, it went straight at and took it at one bound; which was the light, and which the heavy artillery?

A case so glaring as that of Trautenau may actually not have occurred again in the Campaign; but on no occasion did the artillery play a conspicuous part; individual batteries at Nachod and Skalitz, no doubt, showed a great deal of artilleristic courage; true, at the commencement of the first battle the conditions would only allow of a partial employment of the artillery; but it can never be said that the artillery manœuvred at all, the most it did was to hold its own against the Austrian artillery till the end of the battle.

At Koniggrätz, as we have already said, the Prussian artillery of the first army did nothing, but there was no want of room to have planted a greater number of guns than the Austrians, for from Ober-Dohalitz to Trisowitz is some 4,000 paces. But it may be objected that these batteries would have had their line of retreat cut off by the river Bistritz, and would have been obliged to have ascended singly from behind the wood of Sadowa under the overwhelming fire of the Austrians. But then, why were not as many bridges thrown over the Bistritz as the materials would allow? For what purpose are pioneer battalions? It was easily to be seen, early in the morning, that there would be a long halt here, and how disadvantageous the narrow defile near Sadowa would prove. Or, was the possibility of throwing bridges over the Bistritz considered to be so out of the question on account of its swollen condition, that it was not worth a moment's consideration? If so, then pioneers are useless, their power of constructing bridges ceasing at the very time that it is most necessary to exercise it.

Here was a splendid opportunity for an artillery General to overcome all difficulties, and to bring into play the full resources of the whole of his artillery reserve; certainly it was a very difficult task, but the leader of the artillery in such an army should be a General of the first class.

A still more trivial part than this at Sadowa was played by the artillery of the Elbe Army. It never did anything more than exchange shots with the enemy, who occupied a defensive position at a distance of from 4,000 to 5,000 paces.

The excellent conduct of some individual batteries does not invalidate this judgment. Artillery operations on a grand scale are not made up by adding together the independent prowess of individual batteries; they should be carried out according to proper laws and large views. But many materially unfavourable conditions, such as a large number of smooth-bore guns, and being constrained generally to take the offensive against the Austrian artillery, well planted in defensive positions, required an unusual exertion of the talented element in tactics.

There will not be found many voices, even among artillerists, who can assert that they are contented with the work of the artillery in the last campaign. The question is much too important, too critical, to be here palliated on account of respectful considerations. The tactical, not the technical, training of the artillery, will have a decisive influence on the next campaign. What is the use of an artillery which makes capital practice indeed, but which is never in the right place? Much better, one that blazes away cheerily; that at any rate rejoices the hearts of the men.

Is the tactical training, then, of our artillery a sufficient one?

It would be very fortunate if competent judges could answer this question in the affirmative. But with regard to this the only competent decision will be found in the battles of the next war.

9

Influence of the Artillery on the battles of the future – Escorts – Principles for the formation of orders of battle

In future it will only be possible for infantry to storm a position when aided by the fire of a powerful artillery. To this end it is necessary that the batteries should be extended far from the centre on each wing. An artillery which is posted in the centre before the attacking columns loses the possibility of suddenly deploying its whole force; it is stinted as to room, and will in most, cases be obliged to cease firing at the moment that the infantry advances, and causes the whole fire of the enemy to be concentrated on the most sensitive part. The considerable distance of individual batteries does not prevent their working in common with the rest, and on the sane point, while their position on the wings allows of their throwing in a flanking fire. In this position, however, they are necessarily exposed to danger, and, from a vague fear that the guns may be taken, they are often allowed uselessly and inoperatively to cling to the brigade. Artillery should, however, be made use of so as to be able to work together with the infantry, and yet immediately to cease that connection and act independently. To this end we (Prussians) must alter our system of escort to the guns.

Up to this time our escorts have been given, according as it is laid down in trip regulations, on the most different plans, through which one fundamental principle shows itself, viz the general desire to get rid of this disagreeable service as cheaply as possible. In some cases a detachment, composed of men taken from all the six battalions of the brigade, with one officer per regiment to command, forms the escort; a plan which is worthless as having no inner stay, but which breaks up the order of the infantry as little as possible; in other cases individual subdivisions are made use of much to the disgust of the captains of companies. Then, at times, whole companies are told off for this duty who go to their thankless and troublesome work in anything but a good humour. Even squadrons have been thus employed, but only as a matter of form or from a vague feeling that they must be employed somehow. But how can a squadron ever perform this purely defensive duty? If it should charge an attacking squadron, the battery remains without any support, an infantry attack being quite overlooked; moreover, even pioneer companies have been put to this duty. The immediate inventor of this hussar practical joke certainly must have been very proud of it, and the pioneers themselves entered into it with a kind of wild inspiration. Here was a brilliant future for them, in comparison with their otherwise ordinary modest duties. But this is making use of a force for a purpose for which it was never intended.

When the ability to allow a battery great freedom of movement is appreciated, it will be seen that the principle, which should guide the selection of an escort, is only that it may give a feeling of perfect security, and then a different principle will be adopted.

We have a corps in the army whose selected material makes it fit for the most arduous duties, and which possesses an essentially defensive power, that is, the Jägers. In the general model of the infantry it is certainly difficult to admit any special corps, and thus we see the Jägers made use of like the rest; not unfrequently the whole four companies are together in battalion. The excellent qualities for which the Jägers are distinguished permitted them to supply that which was wanting in themselves for that, kind of service, and even enabled them to accomplish with great ability that which was contrary to their special training. But by employing them thus their best power is thrown away. To use Jäger companies as a baggage escort cannot be a proper employment for them. This speciality is so disproportionately small, that it will be well only to employ them on the more important services where their intrinsic worth and great defensive powers can be brought into play. For a Jäger company no more suitable, important, and honourable post can be assigned than that of escort to a battery which is in an exposed position on a wing. If a friendship of association should spring up between the men of such a battery and the Jäger company which is their constant escort, one would then learn to rely upon the other, and thus a surprising freedom of movement would accrue to the battery, while the Jäger company would have a noble opportunity of sustaining the reputation of its special arm. Four four-pounder batteries, with leaders picked out for this special service, might be joined to four Jäger companies, having leaders carefully selected for their personal qualities. The other batteries might have, with the same view, infantry companies told off for their escort. Besides this, it is indispensably necessary to post with every battery from half to a whole troop of cavalry, in order to clear the ground to the front and flank when the artillery might be required suddenly to move quickly forward or retire, and with which movement the infantry would not be able to keep up for the moment; and during the fire it might take up a position and keep the side of the battery clear. Otherwise, as is now the case, at the word "Trot," the battery leader, with a glance at the despairing faces of the infantry, laboriously trying to take up the pace, must trust to his lucky star. Most certainly some will find themselves considerably put out of temper (sich sträuben) at this "useless" breaking up of battalions and squadrons. "Concentration of force" is the favourite expression of our time; but there is a point when the solicitous keeping together of a force is like the proceeding of a skinflint who has his money stolen because he will not go to the expense of a strong box. If we are to require bold tactical movements from a battery leader, before all things we must put him in a position in which he can feel confidence. These particular supports are not only useful, but in most cases have a direct influence on the battle.

If the attacking side shall have succeeded in establishing a superior artillery, that is, as many batteries as it has at its disposition, the first question to be asked is, which is the point to be attacked? If one battery exchanges shots with one of the enemy's batteries, another with another, and the third fires on an occupied field-work, while the fourth thinks that it has discovered the position of the enemy's reserve, we cannot call this an artillery action having a common purpose. To silence the artillery of the enemy cannot be the most important object of the side which takes the offensive. Even if this should be done, the advance of the infantry on a position defended by breech-loaders is not possible. To silence the attacking guns is the essential object of the artillery on the defensive, then the infantry will know how to repulse the attack of the enemy's infantry; but artillery on the offensive should, on the contrary, make it the principal object to play upon the infantry of the enemy. An attack can only be thought of when this has been weakened. It has only to engage with the artillery of the defensive in so far as is absolutely necessary, always having the principal object in view.

It will depend upon the whole disposition of the battle, on which point of the enemy's formation the decisive attack lies. The officer commanding the attack has nothing more to do than to indicate to the nearest batteries where he considers this point to be, and then the rest will direct their fire at the same, in as great a measure as their occupation with the enemy's artillery will allow them. The point of attack need not be especially pointed out to the infantry, for it will, by natural instinct, make its efforts at that point which the artillery has opened out and made easy for it. At the right moment, all the troops, however separately placed, will hasten to the attack. The infantry which hurries to the assault has not much to fear from the enemy's artillery, provided the advance be made quickly and unexpectedly. The artillery, on the side of the offensive, with the present arms of precision, will continue its fire till the moment of the shock with the enemy, after which it may fire over the heads of the whole into the enemy's reserves.

Perhaps it may be here objected that all this is nothing new, and that it may be found in any book on tactics. This we admit; and further, we remember that it was to this very manœouvre that we owe the brilliant success of Duppel. But the Campaign of 1866 shows no analogous example. The condition – breech-loader against muzzleloader – caused such a careful preparatory proceeding to appear superfluous, but when there is an equality of arms on both sides, these manœuvres will reassume their old importance, in a more decided manner.

A mere knowledge, however, of this lever of victory is no warrant for success. A reciprocal action like this of the two arms cannot be commanded mechanically at will.

As the whole method of infantry fighting which we have spoken of requires, as a necessary condition, the individual training of the soldier, as well as his officer, and as a badly formed army will never be in a position to reap the full advantages of the breech-loader, it follows, that in such an admixture of infantry and artillery tactics, a high degree of tactical training is required on the part of the officers of both these services, and it is only in bodies of officers of the greatest military ability that individuals be found equal to the occasion. The General commanding can only define the decisive point, and order a suitable advance of the infantry in the proper direction. From that time forward he must rely on the tact and bravery of his subordinate leaders, while he exercises a general superintendence, taking advantage of anything that may have been gained, and hastening to retrieve any disadvantageous repulse. At the decisive moment all forms and connections are dissolved, and the unfettered power of the individual works alone. When the object has been gained, orders and forms resume their rights again with still greater strictness.

That army will chain victory to its colours which can without danger afford to relax these forms for a moment, because it will then feel sure that all its unchained power will still work with its whole force in one direction, and that it can at any moment be again brought back into the old channel of obedience.

Wars are no longer decided by numbers and the favour of fortune, but rather by the greater individual worth of the armies, and hence of the nations from which they are supplied.

The concentrated action of great masses of artillery has become an axiom since the times of Napoleon. In order to realize this principle, it has been thought necessary to keep all the artillery massed together out of the reach of the fire. But results have shown that this placing the artillery together in large masses, instead of guaranteeing its mutual action, not only throws continual difficulties in the way, but also necessarily leads to a disruption of the order of battle. With us (Prussians) the artillery of an infantry division has no post told off for particular brigades; yet the case of a brigade operating without artillery is scarcely conceivable. The numerous artillery of a corps d'armée dragging on behind the whole body may perhaps meet with defective ground, and thus be precluded from coming into action at all. A greater distribution of the unwieldy masses will, in most cases, greatly facilitate their movement, and there can be very little difficulty in concentrating them again. At the decisive moment indeed, the detached parts can all unite, and the idea that one portion of the army, with its artillery detained somewhere, can be left out and not be able to share the action, may be met by the fact that very often the whole reserve artillery concentrated into one mass fails to come into action at all.

Here perhaps would be the place to go more deeply into the reasons which have misled us entirely in our primitive formation of these great masses of artillery, and (as will be hereafter shown) of cavalry, in the original order of battle. Strategy offers us a very intelligible analogy, and for that reason should be here stated.

The fundamental strategic principle of Napoleon, to which he owed his victories, was the concentration on the decisive point of the largest possible masses of troops. That fact in itself would soon have been acknowledged; but it was often perfectly lost sight of, that the method of accomplishing this was the very thing which constituted his genius. It was thought possible to gain by fixed forms that which genius alone can accomplish, and this was the reasoning employed: "In order to have all they disposable force together in the decisive battle it is simply necessary to keep them all together and never to let them separate at all; thus it will be very certain that all will be together on the decisive day. And this was supposed to be a universal formula. But a large army which is kept concentrated for any length of time is its own worst enemy. Large masses will only be moved and provided for with the greatest difficulty. They would soon be forced to separate in order that they might exist. The fundamental principle should rather be to keep the masses as long as possible separated: unite them only at the decisive moment and then again separate them when the object is gained. The decisive moment, however, cannot be fixed by any rule; to seize on it is the work of genius, which ignores all rules. Austria and Prussia offer examples in 1866, which may be considered as excellent models. The Austrian army concentrated itself at Olmutz, in order that, if the enemy should advance into Bohemia, it might move against it; but it was kept concentrated even on the march, so that at any moment it might be ready to join in the battle. The Prussian army advanced separately from four different directions. If the united Austrian army had managed to meet these divisions singly, its strategy would have been triumphant. It merely acted according to the dictates of common sense; but the Prussian strategy was based on the hope of success, and on being able to seize the right moment for concentrating its forces, which is only to be discerned instinctively, and which defies all rules. Those, however, who do not venture to trust to genius, however much it may sometimes be subject to error, will do well to act according to forms and rule; but if these lifeless forms ever come in contact with the true living spirit, they will most certainly be annihilated.

The Napoleonic tactics show the principle very clearly; large cavalry and artillery forces are seen in perfect working order, and it is then concluded that these have only to be massed together in order to secure the victory on the battlefield; but Napoleon only formed such masses when he had leaders qualified to command them, and thus the leader was the spirit, the essential agent, for whom the masses were created; at other times they were only formed and massed on the field for the immediate occasion. And here was the great difficulty, rightly to discern the moment when a great mass of guns should be placed together for a time, and when they should be separated again. If we were to try to reduce the inspirations of genius to rule, and thus secure success, we might indeed transport large cumbersome masses into action securely enough; but when once there, we should perhaps be obliged to separate them again in order to utilize them.

The following study of the cavalry will furnish proofs of the preceding remarks, and will give us an opportunity occasionally to refer to our fundamental principles.

10

On the action of the Cavalry in 1866

To the reciprocal action of the infantry and artillery of which we have hitherto spoken we must now add another agent, the cavalry.

Even the cavalry themselves would hardly wish us to acknowledge their general efficiency in the Campaign of 1866. If they should think that their prowess on that occasion was the best of which they were capable, they may prepare to sing their funeral dirge.

The gravest impeachments of the disproportional backwardness (zurucktreten) of the cavalry are fully borne out by the brilliant individual fights of Nachod, Tobitschau, and Rokeinitz. These affairs prove the possibility of an efficient co-operation on the part of the cavalry; the material is good, and at the same time it is apparent that the opportunity is there, if it is taken at the critical moment. Infantry and artillery are obliged frequently to await the occasion: the cavalry can and should make it; that is, by great and zealous efforts, should force it on (erjagen) for itself.

In speaking of the action of cavalry, we must distinguish between divisional cavalry and the cavalry division; the first has to work in immediate connection with the other branches of its division: the latter – the cavalry division – as an independent tactical body stands more frequently in a strategical, rather than a tactical connection with the rest of the army.

In the last campaign we made the greatest sacrifices, in order to possess these large masses of cavalry. The corps d'armée were provided only in the most sparing degree with cavalry, and, as it afterwards appeared, in insufficient numbers. Great masses of horse were kept together continually in spite of the difficulties of feeding and moving them. Cavalry opportunities occurred such as are seldom met with in the history of wars, a totally defeated army had to retreat without any reinforcements for more than thirty (German) miles over a favourable cavalry ground where there was no strong position: and what was the result?

Only once did the cavalry find an occasion which, according to their judgment, was a fit opportunity, and that was on the 15th July, 1866, at Rokeinitz. The infantry had here broken through one of the enemy's retiring columns, the cavalry division passed through the gap thus made, and throwing themselves upon the second column of the enemy took them by surprise. But of the twenty-four squadrons which had been kept together with such pains throughout the whole campaign, there were only seven that came into action at this decisive spot! a number which might have been brought together, without much difficulty, from the divisional cavalry. Let the reasons be what they may, at any rate it is quite clear, that massing the cavalry together out of the fight is no security for their combined action in the fight.

The posting of the cavalry corps of the first army in its advance into Bohemia, in the rear instead of at the head of the army, according to the spirit of the Napoleonic custom for cavalry masses, may have been caused less on account of the difficulty of the ground, than from a wish to prevent a possible check to it at the commencement. It was thought, preferable to employ the infantry, whose success was considered more sure, though it required more labour, and was less extensive. At any rate, these reasons are very plausible.

But it led finally to this result, that on the 2nd July we were altogether in the dark as to the whereabouts of the enemy's army, which was concentrated opposite to us at the distance of only one (German) mile. In this situation, if the cavalry had only done their duty in the least degree – if a cavalry regiment had been sent forward in all the principal directions, with orders to proceed till they came either upon the Elbe or the enemy's infantry – we certainly should have gained that information which, as it happened, was mainly owing to chance.

Reconnaissances, such as these, are essentially the business of the reserve cavalry, not of the divisional cavalry; and on this occasion they were the more indicated, as we had always to keep in view our communications with the approaching army of the Crown Prince. We were not in a position to make our dispositions solely with regard to our own army. The reasons for these proceedings cannot now be precisely explained; but the fact is self-evident, and cannot be denied.

The action of the cavalry corps on the day of battle did not go beyond the limits of the service of divisional cavalry; the few regiments which attacked, merely acted in this manner. The cavalry division of the second army, as we see from the official account, was not allowed by the reserve artillery of the first army corps to pass, and thus it followed in the rear of the whole. It seems as if it were a kind of irony of destiny that the first army corps was always unlucky in what it did, as well as in what it omitted; it must be ascribed to this corps, that it paralyzed the action of this cavalry division, and thus it may be considered responsible for what the others omitted to do. As to how far the conduct of the cavalry on the 3rd July was influenced by personal considerations, is not to be judged of at present – this will devolve upon history. The duty of the present time is to draw useful conclusions from uncontroverted matters of fact, by comparing them with those of past times. The fame of the Prussian cavalry was established in the Seven Years War. The bare name of Seidlitz has, even now, such influence over the imagination of the soldier, that involuntarily he sees, in his mind's eye, flying masses of infantry pursued by the cavalry which, completing the commencing disorder of the enemy, reaps the harvest which the other arms have sown for them. This imagination takes definite shapes whether we will or not. We see Ziethen stationed with twenty-five squadrons behind the wood of Popowitz. No one asks how he got there, but we are convinced that, it could not be otherwise, for nothing could prevent him from making his way thither. And at the moment in which Seidlitz with his thirty squadrons debouches at Dohalitz, Ziethen also appears. But when we have come again to our sober senses, we simply say that it is too much to require of destiny that the great events of two centuries should be reproduced on the same spot.

After the battle of Koniggräitz, we lost the traces (fuhlung) of the defeated enemy. It would be easy to give a variety of reasons for the general suspension of activity the next day, but it is better simply to acknowledge that the suddenness of the victory benumbed our powers for the moment.

The success, for the accomplishment of which we had put forward our best powers, surprised us finally by its magnitude. There is a modesty in it of which we need not he ashamed, even if we calculated falsely. We had gone into the field with a perfect self-confidence indeed, but also with a respect for the enemy which we had just conquered. Involuntarily we still had a respect for him, even after the victory.

This peculiar insecurity of the army, after the battle, shows most particularly the inactivity of the cavalry. A cavalry accustomed to war would probably have utilized the situation of the 4th on its own account. An independent cavalry leader would take his directions rather from the enemy than front his General. On the 5th this cavalry corps followed in the second line, while the cavalry division of the second army alone took the hand, and crossed the Elbe. The command of this division was given to the army corps which followed it, and after it had at length succeeded in coining up with the enemy at Zwittau, it was obliged to give up the pursuit, as the corps which was behind had taken another line of march. On the 14th it again came up with the enemy. The 15th has been already described. With this first action of the cavalry division, in which it acted as a division, its activity ceased. True it remained from this time at the head of the army, but without showing any important activity. The cavalry corps of the first army was not employed at all; the advance of the united armies, commencing from the 7th, was so energetic that it was impossible for it to take the lead of the infantry.

The action of the divisional cavalry appears generally in a more favourable light. That proves, as we have already remarked, that the material is good, and able to perform all that is required of it. But, by putting together a mosaic work of small cavalry affairs, we can never constitute great cavalry operations. The deeds of a Seidlitz must be conceived in a Seidlitzian spirit.

11

Importance and action of the Cavalry in future Campaigns

We may gather from the history of the wars of former times, that the efficiency of large cavalry masses depends on their leader. A cavalry leader cannot be guided by special orders; he is a General among generals of the highest grade, and should know how to obviate all difficulties which stand in the way of his efficiency. The moment when he should use energetic measures passes away quickly, so that any counsel, except that within his own breast, would be too late. A man such as is required is not necessarily to be found at all times in an army. Genius is not a frequent gift. It is only, however, when a born cavalry General is to be had, that the formation of large masses of cavalry is justifiable; they are not absolutely necessary; but, if a mistake should be made, and the massed cavalry delivered into the hands of one who afterwards is found unfit to command them, the army would be robbed of the co-operation of a powerful agent. A mass of cavalry which remains idle would perhaps have performed good service if it had been separated into smaller divisions. If, not being able to reckon on a born cavalry General, we advocate the distribution of the cavalry by brigades to an army corps, it must not thereby be understood that we renounce altogether the operating by large cavalry masses. On the day of battle the different corps d'armée must always form a junction, and the assembly of the several cavalry brigades of each, so as to form a cavalry division, can be attended with little difficulty. If the constant concentration of the cavalry is found not to secure their common action on the day of battle, as was proved at Koniggrätz and Rokeinitz, perhaps the opposite method of forming the cavalry division on the battlefield will give a better chance of success. The brigade Wnuck was formed for the first time on the day of the battle from different army corps, which, however, did not at all militate against its brilliant efficiency. This method may obviate further the very considerable difficulty of maintenance, &c., and possibly also very hazardous personal questions. In the formation of the original order of battle the chief command of the cavalry is only in competition between the oldest, Generals of that branch – perhaps very able and meritorious officers – but who may be, nevertheless, wanting in the peculiar talent necessary for the command of large masses. If the divisions and corps of cavalry are formed on the spot, it will be easy to choose the officer to command from among those who may be considered the most worthy of confidence. A young General in such a position would then only think of using well the opportunity of gathering his laurels, which might not again occur to him during his lifetime.

Whether the cavalry will be able to play an especially prominent part in future wars, may be decided by the experiences of 1866, as well from what did happen as from what did not. So long as rapidity, boldness, and dash (Waghalsigkeit) are active agents in war, the cavalry will retain its importance. A cavalry devoid of these qualities, but merely possessing good intentions, obedience, with ordinary bravery (hausbackener tapferkeit) and a laudable modesty (löblicher bescheidenheit),[1] is worse than none at all. In the last century, even when the firearms were not to be compared to those of the present day, the cavalry were never supposed to attack unshaken infantry, or to move within grapeshot range of batteries. Then, also, it was well understood that they must watch their opportunity. These conditions have altered very little. If the greater range of the firearms of the present day obliges the cavalry to keep their distance, at the same time the "terrein coupé" on which battles are now fought will afford them many opportunities for a nearer approach under cover, without acting disadvantageously on their efficiency. But the cavalry must learn to accustom itself to the new feature in war of the trenched and broken ground, and not demand plains, on which firearms can be used against them with the greatest advantage. A lighter cavalry is required, and not a heavy one.

The proper place for the cavalry is a considerable distance at the head of the advancing column, where, if possible, they should be distributed by regiments, to gain information, to keep up the communication with neighbouring corps d'armée, and thus bring cohesion and security to the whole body. During the fight a similar rôle falls to their share. They should look to the security of the wings, and endeavour to turn those of the enemy. Trautenau affords an example of this. If the Prussians had had their head the whole of the cavalry brigade of twelve squadrons which was present, they would easily have been ably to drive back the Austrian cavalry behind Hohenbruck as they debouched from the town, to the west of which they were stationed, whereas the few squadrons of dragoons who were at hand were not in sufficient force to master them. The place of the cavalry brigade clearly was here in the front, in order to watch the progress of the battle. Here it would have been able to have observed and threatened the advance of the Austrian brigade on the chaussée of Burkersdorf; its retreat never could have been endangered. Instead of this, during the whole of the fight it remained to the eastward of the town with the Aupa before it, and heights, formed by almost inaccessible rocks, which men on foot could only climb with difficulty. Posted as they were, their purpose could only have been, to join the rest of the troops at the proper moment, on their advance or retreat. Further, if a cavalry regiment had been sent forward to the left wing of the

1 Whoever heard of a modest dragoon? – *Translator*

eight battalions of the second division in the direction of Alt-Rognitz to Rudersdorf, the attack on the left wing would have been discovered at an early hour, and an uninterrupted communication with the first division of the Guards would have been rendered possible. The most insignificant demonstration in that direction would have brought the Austrian attack to a stand.

The thin and extended lines of formation in battle will, in future, afford the cavalry opportunities of acting in a new aspect, by giving it occasions for energetic and immediate co-operation with the infantry and artillery in action. If the infantry works with the cavalry at hand, the latter will then be in a position to take advantage of the decisive moment, which has been prepared for it by the artillery, and the present tactics with regard to skirmishers which require swarms of men in loose order will reap the richest advantages. It will not be impossible for them to throw themselves through gaps in the enemy's line on their reserve; and even if no success were to follow, they would still spread terror and consternation. Indeed the moral effect that an efficient fire of musketry or shell always makes even on the best infantry, causes a favourable opportunity to arise for the use of the cavalry. By an independent action the horse-artillery can now prepare an attack at a far more effective distance than formerly.

The cavalryman of the present time must not shrink from the common law, which requires that he shall manifest his individual qualities. He should be more of a partisan (parleigänger).[2] Freedom of judgment should be required of him which will fit him to judge of the whole current of the battle, and to know how to attack at the right places and at the proper moment. No cavalryman should be ordered to manœuvre on the flanks or in the rear; he himself must judge when he should do so. He should also know the weak points of the other arms so as to support them, and their strong points in order to draw advantage from them.

Our cavalry altogether is still upon its trial; but we have no reason to look with mistrust on the issue.

2 Note: i.e. designed to carry on a desultory warfare. *Translator*

12

Cooperation of the Engineers

It now remains for us to cast a glance on the action of the fourth arm in the campaign, the engineers. It is a strange circumstance that the two very branches of the army which played so important a part in the Campaign of 1864, the artillery and engineers, should fall so much into the shade in that of 1866. On the part of the artillery this may be explained by a disproportionate preponderance of its technical over its tactical training, a fault in artillery which can never be too much denounced. An excuse may be suggested for the engineer, that the very rapid offensive operations of the campaign afforded neither time nor opportunity for his co-operation, which is always essentially of a defensive nature. These views would nevertheless rest upon a mistaken notion of the facts of every battle, and also of the proper duties of the engineers themselves.

Pioneers were left behind at the rear halting-places by preference; thus at Reichenberg three companies were employed as a baggage guard, which at once shows that the services of a company of infantry were prized higher for the battle than one of pioneers; the latter, however, were at times used as infantry in action, in order to make them in some manner useful. Thus they followed in the retinue of the army, au encumbrance which every one sought to get rid of with as good a grace as possible. What officer of engineers can say that he feels satisfied with the action of his arm in the campaign?

We cannot here refrain from a little anecdote:

An officer of engineers had formed the praiseworthy wish to hear, at any rate once, the whizzing of a shell, but he waited in vain for an opportunity, till the middle of July. At this time his division was before Olmutz; one day a shell came from the fortress – a veritable, bodily shell, and flew whizzing right over the cantonments of the pioneers; but, poor fellow! that very afternoon he had got a few hours' leave of absence, and when he returned, he learnt that it had been there, but, like "The maiden from foreign parts,"[1] it had vanished and left not a trace behind. Deep sense often lies in a childish tale.

According to Prussian ideas, intrenchments had fallen into disrepute. They were thought to be detrimental to that offensive spirit which was the leading principle in our conduct of the war. The example of that of the Austrians led us to scout the idea; but we rejected the good with the bad. (Man

1 A comparison from Schiller's "Mädchen aus der Fremde."

schüttet aber hier das Kind mit dem Bade aus.) The fault of the Austrians was, that they threw up their intrenchments beforehand, and then expected that the fight would take such a course as would render them useful. Instead of making the fight dependent on the intrenchments, we would make the intrenchments dependent on the fight. For the possibility of doing this, we would refer to the situation of the first army on the 3rd of July, at from 8 to 2 o'clock. Against the well-posted Austrian artillery we could make no sufficient head with our own; we plainly saw that we should be obliged to hold the position till the coming up of the second army either obliged the enemy to retreat, or at least diverted so much of its force as would enable us to take the offensive. The last was the most probable. Was it not, then, apparent that we ought, favoured as we were by mist and rain, to throw up, by means of the pioneers, épaulements for as many guns as we had room for, at 2,000 paces, opposite to the enemy's line of fire? It would only have taken two hours, or till 11 o'clock, to complete them all. Even if the Austrians, in spite of the fog which partially covered the position, had fired upon our long and thin lines before we could obtain sufficient cover, the work might have been rendered more difficult, but it would not altogether have been prevented. An attempt would certainly have been worthwhile, in order to have gained a decided preponderance, without being reduced to depend upon the second army, whose success was by no means certain. The artillery of the Elbe Army was in a precisely similar situation, although it had no opportunity of developing itself, for there the woods would have greatly facilitated the rapid construction of épaulements on their borders, into which the batteries brought by the road through the wood could have been immediately placed and brought into action. Thus we ought to have fortified the borders of the wood at Sadowa, in order to have been prepared for an attack from the Austrians.

In a still more decided manner might the pioneers have operated at Trautenau. As the retreat of the battalions scattered from Hohenbruck to Alt-Rognitz could be no longer doubtful, and as we were aware that, as far to the rear as the Aupa, there was no reserve worth mentioning present to relieve the hard-pressed troops; an intrenched battery on the Kappellenberg, or, still better, épaulements on the heights of North Krieblitz (for the construction of which there was ample time), would have supplied the want of these reserves, and without any doubt have reestablished the battle. But there were no pioneers, we had left them behind, though even there the same evening they might have co-operated in a most efficient manner. As, from time to time, the troops were driven down from the hills to the east of the town into the vale of the Aupa – an event which might have been foreseen for hours before – it was most important that the corps should occupy a defensive position, à cheval, on the road to Lebau, to the north of Parschnitz, and pass the night in front of the defile, in order to be ready the next morning to co-operate again with the garde corps. If we had immediately thrown up épaulements for our ninety-six guns at the defensive position selected, and occupied them with the reserve artillery on the spot, under the protection of the five intact battalions, the position would have been impregnable, and the retreating troops could have been reformed behind it without danger. There was abundant time to have done this. But perhaps the soldiers were not sufficiently engineers, or the engineers soldiers enough, for this consideration to slave entered into their thoughts.

The engineer, in virtue of the character which is particular to his branch of the service, may hold an equilibrium in military operations. He may render the success gained by an impetuous attack secure, by quickly throwing up field-works (Banten) behind the attacking force, and in the same manner stop a retreat by hastily constructed intrenchments, the holding of which then concerns the honour of the troops.

But it is not only by defensive, but also by offensive measures that the engineer can operate most effectually. It has been already shown what an important influence a number of bridges thrown over the Bistritz might have had. They would have permitted of a simultaneous establishment of the artillery, and made their supplies secure, have facilitated the carrying of the wounded to the rear, and aided towards a general appearance of the cavalry on the scene. In short, the never-ending difficulty of the crowded bridge at Sadowa would have been obviated. It is altogether incredible, considering the number of pioneers that were on the spot, that the idea was never entertained of constructing these bridges. But the official account does not mention that such an operation was ever proposed, much less attempted. This omission, however, might have been most disastrous to the troops which advanced, had they been obliged to retreat, a contingency which ought always to be taken into the reckoning. Swollen water and swampy banks cannot possibly justify the omission; for we should then be tempted to ask, for what purpose are the pioneers, if they are unable to build a bridge over a swollen river? for were the water low, no bridge would be required.

Precisely similar circumstances appear if we turn to the Elbe Army. The defiling through Mechanitz was brought to a stand, because the head of the column of the sixteenth division alone was four hours and a half about it. It is difficult to believe that in that time a second passage could not have been established, even if only for the infantry, which would then have enabled the division to take a more decisive part in the action.

If we take a review of the battles of the campaign in this point of view, we shall find that there were frequent occasions when the action of the engineers might have been useful. The reasons why that branch of the service was less active than the other may be found in the remark, that they were both equally in fault. The services of the engineers were so little appreciated that it was not considered worthwhile to request their co-operation, so that, however willing, they could not take their part in the works. But is it not also a fault in the engineer himself when the tactician and the soldier is subordinated to the mere architect and constructor?

An engineer, who employs all his time in fortifications, exchanges voluntarily the position of a soldier for that of an artisan. An engineer, who is a good soldier and an indifferent architect, will always be serviceable, even though his constructions may in a measure fail in an artistic point of view. An indifferent construction at the right place is better than an artistic work at the wrong one. The great importance of the commanding engineer in an army can only be appreciated when we see him at the side of the General Commanding-in-Chief, superintending the whole strategic and tactical position, and seizing the opportunity when his own branch of the service can advantageously and actively operate in the battle. The actual carrying out of the work may always be left to subordinates: details easily confuse.

The next campaign will show us this fourth arm acting in rivalry with the others in the battle.

13

Necessity of a critical examination of lost battles

In the foregoing chapters we have endeavoured to explain how the mutual action of the different arms did not always fulfil just tactical principles in the battles of the Campaign of 1866. We have further tried to show how the excellence of the infantry, and the superiority of its arm, together with a determined and circumspect leading, compensated entirely for all these disadvantages. In an examination of these infantry tactics, as they were developed by the peculiarity of the troops and the properties of their arm, we may see that they contain not only the elements of victory, but also especially the germs of defeat, if the proper limits are overstepped.

In the almost uninterrupted course of victory in this campaign, we can only point to two failures, at Trautenau and Langensalza, and we feel convinced that a critical examination of these two battles must reveal the weak point. Such a task is not only instructive and useful, but it is also a duty towards those on whose shoulders the responsibility will rest of commanding troops in future battles.

The reason is very easily explained why we avoid as much as possible entering into these difficult questions. Consideration for the reputation of many excellent persons, whom we ought not and do not wish to injure, restrict so sensibly a judgment which we wish to be free and unbiased, that, for the present at least, a truly instructive view, a free statement of reasons and actions, might by many persons be considered impracticable. But the times are serious, and render a most earnest examination imperative. The facts themselves cannot be denied: they belong to history. Of what use could it be if we were to be obstinately silent concerning them? Even were we to attempt to cast the mantle of oblivion over them, it would only deceive men of little discernment, who perhaps might not be able to see through it. But those of better judgment would rend it away, and the bitter criticism of enmity would be the more severe, inasmuch as it would have just grounds for its strictures. By silence, moreover, we rob ourselves of an important means of instruction, which is another very great disadvantage. Wherever there is action, there also a cause is always to be found, and when the question is a lost battle, it is not difficult to see that there must have been an error somewhere. Disgrace, however, only attaches to those leaders or troops who can be accused of misbehaviour and cowardice. If, however, the cause of failure lies in another direction, for instance in a faulty leading, it is certainly very painful for those concerned, but not dishonourable.

Such things are purposely kept in semi-obscurity, in which the outlines are only seen indistinctly. No one is accused; of course it was only a series of misunderstandings, and we hear the softly whispered suggestion that the troops engaged were not to be compared with the rest. That posterity will hereafter come to a proper conclusion is a very poor consolation. The living also have their rights.

To be able to ascertain how far the unfortunate result of a battle can be ascribed to tactical errors, it is necessary to give a picture of the fight drawn in broad lines both as to causes and effects.

14

On the battle of Trautenau

We will now take into our consideration the affair at Trautenau. In the foregoing chapters occasion has been taken several times to refer to individual episodes of this action. The official accounts describe it in broad characters, and we premise that all are well acquainted with these.

At the very beginning of the action a misunderstanding arose. On the 27th the two divisions advanced on Trautenau by the roads of Lebau and Schomberg. To the first division was assigned in orders, the occupying of the defile of Trautenau; in consequence of which the officer commanding the second division, which by chance arrived two hours before the first, did not consider it his duty to occupy it, and therefore waited till the first arrived, which it did at dearly the same time as the Austrian brigade Mondel, from the opposite direction.

Notwithstanding this, it did not follow that the misunderstanding should necessarily be attended with serious consequences. The engagement commenced. Our aim was to hurl back this Austrian brigade, and then to march and occupy Arnau with the whole corps, according to orders. The avant garde, seven battalions strong, engaged on the right wing, to the south and south-west of the town, the eight battalions of the second division were directed to the hills on the east of the town. Thus there still remained ten disposable battalions.

The mode in which the individual companies of the avant garde were placed in the line of battle according to the official account involves the most serious considerations. It would be well to examine whether such an intricate mixing up of the troops, such a departure from the ordre de bataille of the first formation as was here practised without any reason, might not have been avoided; this we say notwithstanding our assertion in a former chapter that in the course of a battle the strict observance of the order of battle is, often only possible at the expense of its success.

The choice of the eight battalions of the second division from the centre, as well as the manner and character of their leading in action, necessarily had the effect of rendering all united action impossible.

About three o'clock the object of the action was gained, and the Austrian brigade beaten back in the direction of New Rognitz. The troops thought that the affair was at an end. The officer commanding, who had remained in the town, had not till this moment attached much importance to the engagement. His view was to continue the march to Arnau, according to his orders. The avant garde had assembled in the town; the ten battalions of infantry, which were not engaged, and the whole of the cavalry and artillery, were to the eastward of the town in the valley of the Aupa. The eight battalions alone of the second division deployed in a thin line more than 2,000 paces long, proceeding over broken ground, often fell into disorder; and at length found themselves between Hohenbruck and Alt-Rognitz, 2,000 paces to the south-ward of the town, and cut off from it by steep mountains, difficult of access, so that an engagement might have happened without being at all noticed by those in the town. They had neither cavalry nor artillery with them.

About half-past four o'clock, Gablentz, with three brigades, approaching in the direction of the western exit of Alt-Rognitz, met these weak lines at the same time that the brigade Mondel sought again to take the offensive on its left.

It is not difficult to see that these eight battalions must have been forced back in the direction of Kriblitz; they were distant some 2,500 paces from that place, the ground was difficult, it was impossible to see any distance over it, and there were no supports. Notwithstanding this, the retreat was very slow, and it was eight o'clock when they reached the heights to the northward of Kriblitz. There they were received by the battalions of the reserve.

The batteries of the second division re-crossed the Aupa, and again formed to the westward of the exit of Parschnitz. They took up a position in columns from the centre, piled arms and waited. Thus they continued for an hour till darkness came on, the rest of the corps also waiting around them; the noise of the fight had died away; then came the word of command: "Stand to your arms! Shoulder arms! Right about face – march!" The retreat had commenced.

Slowly they approached the entrance to the narrow mountain defiles, through a mass of carriages; it took a long time for each corps to join itself on to the long chain. It was now utterly dark; slowly and in silence the columns marched through the defile ten miles long.

But the corps left success, together with its honour, behind at Parschnitz.

What the reasons were that influenced the General commanding to order this retreat, remains a very difficult question.

The repulse of the eight, battalions, which, on account of the tactics they adopted, had not the necessary power of resistance, was only indirectly of importance, inasmuch as it necessitated the officer commanding the whole to come to an independent decision, which otherwise would have been spared him.

The official report says: –

> The portion of the troops which had retreated, had already taken up their march on the high-road to Parschnitz, which obliged the officer commanding to follow after with the rest.

These "portions" belonged to those eight battalions of the second division, which we have mentioned as having been engaged till eight o'clock in the evening.

The commanding officer of the second division is dead. The expression "portions" is a very vague one; certainly it could only have been small ones, broken-up subdivisions, or companies at the most. The body of the division was at Parschnitz. The ground was not of a nature to permit the troops falling out, and melting away out of the hands of their officers. The whole of the troops were obliged to work themselves through the two long defiles. Late at night some of the troops were still waiting at the entrance. But even if it is admitted that an important part of the division – perhaps half, six battalions – had already, at eight o'clock, got so far to the rear that their recall was beyond the reach of possibility, still there remained nineteen battalions with the officer commanding, as well as the whole of the cavalry and artillery. And yet with these he felt obliged to retire through the defile.

But still this night march in the narrow defile showed that the old Prussian spirit of discipline and obedience was not extinct. No part of the army was put to so severe a test as the first army corps on that night.

From this time forward a dark shadow seemed to hang over this corps. It felt that it had a something to retrieve, for which it had not itself to blame. Fortune seemed inclined to favour it. This corps, on the morning of the 3rd, was the nearest body of the second army to the enemy. Was an opportunity intentionally offered it of retrieving the 27th of June; or was it a happy accident, that it received at an early hour the direct order to engage according to the commanding officer's judgment? But for two long hours the troops, in a state of feverish excitement, listened in their bivouacs to the distant thunder of the cannon. At last came the word of command, "Stand to your arms! Shoulder arms! Take ground to your left – march!" The corps arrived just as the battle was ended!

If afterwards a painful expression might be discerned in the countenances of this corps, does the fact require explanation?

15

On the battle of Langensalza

As for the other unfortunate affair of Langensalza, it appears at first sight that no explanation is necessary: that it was the numerical superiority and not the tactics of the enemy that caused the result. But this, however, is not the ease. This action affords a most instructive example of the weak point in our tactics.

It was quite correct in General Fliess to attack the Hanoverians on the 27th, notwithstanding their great superiority in numbers. It may be objected that, had he only waited one day longer, he would have been joined by a superior force, which would have rendered the results certain; or, perhaps, have avoided any fighting at all. But during this one day the Hanoverians might have made a movement to the northward or eastward, which was the very thing that under the circumstances we were bound to prevent. We had already been too long groping about in uncertainty not to wish to bring the thing to a conclusion, cost what it might; time passed, the Hanoverians must be held fast at Langensalza, or pushed towards the south.

A bare appearance before the front of the Hanoverian position would not have accomplished this purpose. On the contrary, from the indecision which they had up to this time evinced, it would have been reasonable to suppose that they would have withdrawn towards the north in order to avoid a collision. Probably we should have obtained the same results, had we been able to sustain a prolonged battle with less numerous troops. If it was necessary to compel the Hanoverians to retain their position, there was only one way to do so, and that was, by means of an energetic attack, to force their whole line to a serious engagement.

But the Prussian General must have been fully convinced that, with such conditions of strength, he could never think of gaining the victory over the Hanoverians. The utmost in his power was to keep them back on the Unstrut, and thus make a drawn battle. But even if the Hanoverians should take the offensive, and force him to retire on Gotha, this retreat would be far from a lost battle; it would, on the contrary, be a solution of his problem, and thus really a victory. The principal point of view of the Prussian General, throughout the battle, should have been, not to allow the retreat, which he foresaw, to degenerate into a tactical defeat.

If the situation had been properly understood, a strong line of distinction ought to have been drawn between the main body, which should have attacked the enemy with energy, and a strong reserve posted within reach of the battle, towards the rear, with special orders not to take part in the fight, either partially or generally, but to reserve itself for the one purpose of forming a rallying-point, behind which an orderly retreat might have been made along the left road to Gotha.

But the battle really showed a very different aspect from this in its formation, and the reserve was quite unsuitable to these requirements. After a short time, not only the advanced guard, and the main body, but also a part of the weak reserve was engaged in the first line, and the companies were all mixed up one with another in the greatest confusion. Without the slightest necessity one company after another was hurled into the chaos of the fight. Very soon all were swallowed up in the front line, and thus all power of movement was lost. All the guns were engaged in front. This could not have been done with the intention of silencing the Hanoverian fire, and thus preparing an attack for the infantry. The only purpose which could be proposed was, the drawing off the fire of the enemy's artillery from the engaged troops. But for this, one half the number of guns would have been sufficient, the rest were imperatively required for the reserve. But further than this, from the small corps d'armée three companies were detached half a mile (German) on the left flank, for a service which could have been efficiently performed by a squadron, while the weak cavalry was posted in the first line in the rear of the centre.

When the Hanoverians at length attacked these weak lines with superior force, that happened which was inevitable – they were broken, and their component parts driven back. No reserve was at hand, and thus any rallying was impossible. The case was nearly the same as that of Trautenau, and the position of the forces was of a similar nature. This example proves in a very evident manner, like the other, that a deployed line, long exposed to fire, has not sufficient power in itself to resist a vigorous attack, and that it can only prevail by having a strong reserve under the immediate command of the General-in-Chief, in a defensive position in the rear, which will serve to rally the beaten troops, and break the shock of the enemy's columns.

If, however, we take a lesson from these two actions, we shall not have paid too dearly for our experience.

16

Conclusion

Here, then, we close this tactical retrospect. What we have said may suffice to fix attention on those points which are worth noticing. Possibly we may have been mistaken in some of the details, but we only attach importance to the general ideas which may be traced throughout our remarks. If these should be just, the unimportant details of the points mooted, although not exactly correct, certainly cannot make the whole false. There are some, perhaps, who may think us to blame for leaving here spoken openly of circumstances, the truth of which has hitherto been concealed from the public eye. In all classes of society there are, no doubt, questions which should not be brought to open discussion, and which we endeavour to bear and cure in secret; but matters belonging to the history of battles cannot be comprised in this category, Battles cannot be fought secretly. What possible purpose would it serve to hide errors which one day by a signal defeat may be revealed, most intelligibly, to the whole world? But it may be replied that an individual opinion, which is not infallible, may, by spreading false views, do as much harm as it would otherwise do good were its views correct, and thus, to obviate all danger, all individual views should be suppressed. We do not subscribe to this doctrine. He, who thinks that he is able to speak the truth usefully, is justified in so doling. He knows his own responsibility.

But it may also be urged the time is not yet come to publish these things. When, then, will the time come? When those on whom, perhaps, now, an undeserved reproach is cast are dead; when it will probably be too late to profit by the experiences which we have gained. The time has always arrived to speak the truth.

The present times are much too momentous to be regarded with indifference. What turn political combinations will take, whether for war or peace, no man can foretell. The course of events often deceives the most clear-sighted speculations. But when a danger threatens, is it wise to say "Oh, it will not happen, or at any rate not yet"? The war which may break out will be a most serious matter for the soldier. He can and will meet it with the fullest confidence in his powers, which have been already proved. Nevertheless, the most absolute self-examination is necessary. Our army has to thank the circumstance of its earnest training at home for its success up to the present time. In the future it will be far from boasting: "We leave attained perfection," when it is only in the endeavour to reach it that the essence of a healthy life consists.

One conclusion, however, may be drawn from what we have hitherto advanced: In the wars of the future, the decisive element will not be brute force, but rather intellect (geist), not only on the part of the leader, but from him down to the last soldier, and each individual will weigh in the scale according to the whole value of his intellectual individuality. A battle between two armies is nothing more than a struggle between two nations who put forth their best powers to defend that which is most sacred to them; and so long as a nation keeps to the true principles which lead the civilization of man forward in the path of progress, its armies can never be beaten.

Note By The Translator

Trautenau is a town with the river Aupa running past it, several heights command it, and it forms a very strong position. The Prussians were advancing on the side of the town on which the river flows, the Austrians were posted in the opposite direction, and of course their object was to arrest the advance of their opponents. In fact, it was a question which should first occupy the town. The first army corps of the Prussians was bivouacked among the hills, one march distant, and they received orders to occupy Trautenau. They marched in two principal columns, the right and the left. In orders, the right column was detailed to occupy the town as early as possible. It however happened that the left column arrived first, at 8 am, and, finding that the right had not come up, its commanding officers thought proper to wait, as the other column had been ordered to occupy the town. But the right column had been delayed from some cause, and did not arrive till 10 o'clock; these two hours made all the difference, for when they at last came up, they found that part of an Austrian corps had, in a measure, forestalled them, and that the heights commanding the town on the south were in possession of the brigade Mondel. It is impossible, without knowing the exact words of the orders which were given, to say on whose shoulders the blame rests for this misunderstanding. In his able pamphlet on "Responsibility in War," the Archduke Albrecht remarks: –

> In short, every subordinate should, as much as is necessary, be made acquainted with the purport of the orders that are given him; a certain independence, in so far as it does not interfere with the harmonious co-operation of the whole, should be allowed him for the execution of his orders, and he should be made responsible for its exercise.[1]

Now the question is, was the officer commanding the left column acquainted with the general object of the officer commanding the corps, when he received his order to march on the town? For it is possible that had he occupied the town and the heights commanding it, at 8 am, as soon as he arrived, the fortune of the day might have been changed.

If he was not thus informed, the responsibility certainly rests with the officer commanding the first army corps; but also the officer of the left column, had he been a first-class officer should have seen how matters stood, and have occupied the town and heights on his own responsibility, as he must have known that it would be some time before the right column would arrive, and the great importance of its possession must have been sufficiently obvious. But, then, what makes a first-class officer? God makes him, "Nascitur non fit."

HAO

1 "Responsibility in War," p.25. Mitchell and Co.

Playing with the Book